OUTLINING #1

SIZZLING STORY OUTLINES

How to Outline a Novel or Screenplay, Always Know "What Happens Next" When Plotting a Story, and Finish a Draft Without Freaking Out

H. R. D'COSTA

scribemeetsworld.com
Storytelling, Simplified

Copyright 2015, 2016, 2018 H. R. D'Costa. All rights reserved.

First ebook edition published in 2015.

First print edition published in 2018.

Note: This paperback edition contains additional material not included in ebook editions released prior to September 2018.

Because this edition has been specially formatted for print, it may deviate slightly from the current ebook edition.

Cover image is adapted from *Fire Ball 3* by Bert Cash, which is licensed under CC BY 2.0: https://www.flickr.com/photos/bsc_photgraphy/6461699689/.

Various icons provided by iconmonstr.com.

Print edition ISBN: 979-8--50279977-5

Printed in the United States of America

v 1.1

This book is dedicated to my mom and dad.

Thank you for every meal you made me, every ride you gave me, and every lesson you taught me.

Most of all, thank you for supporting my dream to be a writer.

CONTENTS

Introduction 9

PART I
HOW TO MAKE SURE YOUR STORY IDEA
ISN'T A WASTE OF TIME, A.K.A. POPPING
THE STORY KERNEL................................. 27

CHAPTER ONE
Getting Started via the Story Kernel 31

CHAPTER TWO
**Shaping Audience Experience
via SMART Goals and the Protagonist** 37

    Reverse Engineering SMART Goals................39
        Reverse Engineering from Situation 40
        Reverse Engineering from Character 42
        Reverse Engineering from Theme 46
    Can a Protagonist Change His SMART Goal? 48

CHAPTER THREE
**Conjuring Conflict to Entertain Audiences
via the Antagonist**.......................................53

CHAPTER FOUR
**Giving Audiences a Reason to Care About
Your Story via the Stakes** 61

CHAPTER FIVE
Attracting Audiences via Genre 67

v

CHAPTER SIX
Luring Audiences Deeper Still via the Hook......73

5 Surefire Ways to Make
Your Story Idea More Ironic............................81

Irony Combination #1: Most Competency
+ Least Likely..82

Irony Combination #2: Varying Degrees
of Competency + New Waters......................85

Irony Combination #3: Untested Competency
+ Least Likely..88

Irony Combination #4: Competency with Others
+ Incompetency with Self............................91

Irony Combination #5: Attraction + Least Likely.......93

Intrinsic vs. Extrinsic Hooks...........................97

How Hookalicious Does a Story Have to Be?....100

CHAPTER SEVEN
Summarizing Your Story in One Sentence via the Logline......107

PART II
HOW TO BUILD YOUR STORY STRUCTURE, A.K.A. CRACKING YOUR STORY CODE......115

CHAPTER EIGHT
An Overview of Story Structure: The 8 Essential Plot Points of Your Story Outline......121

CHAPTER NINE
Taking Your Story off the Ground via the First-Act Break......131

CHAPTER TEN
Beginning with a Bang via the Inciting Incident and the Opening Image......139

CHAPTER ELEVEN
Swinging Your Story in a New Direction via the Midpoint..................................147

- 8 Ways to Swing Your Story in a New Direction........................ 148
- Matching Your Premise with the Perfect Midpoint............................ 154
- How to Handle Multiple Midpoint Fulcrums 159

CHAPTER TWELVE
Re-Engaging Audience Interest via the Trough ... 163

- Your Master List of Trough Types 165
- Determining an Appropriate Act Two Ending... 166

CHAPTER THIRTEEN
Putting the "Grand" in the Grand Finale via the Climax..175

CHAPTER FOURTEEN
Tying Up Loose Ends via the Resolution........... 183

PART III
HOW TO OUTLINE YOUR STORY WITH A METHOD BACKED BY SCIENTIFIC RESEARCH (SORT OF), A.K.A. EXCAVATING STORY FOSSILS 193

CHAPTER FIFTEEN
An Overview of the Outlining Method...............199

CHAPTER SIXTEEN
The Rationale Behind the Method (The Science Stuff Is Here)........................207

CHAPTER SEVENTEEN

5 Simple Things You Can Do to Secure the Cooperation of Your Creative Genius............213

CHAPTER EIGHTEEN

Frequently Asked Questions About the Method.................................... 225

PART IV
WRAPPING UP...247

CHAPTER NINETEEN

Applying the Finishing Touches to Your Starter Outline............................... 249

CHAPTER TWENTY

Your Convenient Starter Outline Checklist........ 259

CHAPTER TWENTY-ONE

The Method, At Your Service....................... 263

INTRODUCTION

The JOY OF IT. THE THRILL OF IT.

The money, too.

When writing's going well, it can be immensely satisfying, not to mention lucrative.

When it's going well, the words flow freely, and you hammer them out on your keyboard like you're Thor.

But, all too often, this isn't the case.

In the beginning, sure. Enthralled by your story idea, you generate tons of material. Your word count grows in leaps and bounds. But the deeper you get into your screenplay or novel, the more difficult it becomes to write it.

The words no longer flow freely; they trickle out.

Panicked, you stare at your computer screen, wondering, *What happens next?*

You have no clue.

You've run out of steam.

You're stuck.

After several days of not writing anything at all, it dawns on you. You've wasted your precious time on a project that's doomed.

With a sigh of resignation, you stash away your unfinished draft in a storage box, where it joins a host of other false starts.

'Course, you're a writer. You get antsy if you spend too long without writing.

So you try again. This time, you're luckier.

Sort of.

Although you write yourself into a corner again, this time, you manage to write yourself out of it. You don't abandon your draft one-third of the way through.

You finish it.

Even so, you're not terribly keen to celebrate. To be ready to sell, this draft needs restructuring.

Major, major restructuring.

The works.

Scenes, chapters, the last third of your screenplay or novel—thousands of words have to be scrapped—undoing hours, weeks, maybe even months of labor.

When you take stock of your progress, the picture isn't pretty. Your output is dismal when compared to your investment of time. While you're certain the DMV would outscore you on efficiency, you're uncertain whether you'll ever achieve your writing goals.

At this rate, you'll never be able to tell an agent you've got five finished screenplays on hand—which would, hopefully, make you a more enticing prospect to sign on.

At this rate, you won't be able to build up your backlist of novels—which should not only multiply your sources of income but also expand your avenues to market them.

Worse yet, when you're feeling really bleak, you question whether you're even cut out for this writing gig, after all.

Don't lose faith!

The problem probably isn't with you.

The problem is with your method.

You haven't found a way to beat back the beast of the blank page and be as productive as you desire.

Here's one solution to your situation: outline your story before writing it.

And by outline, I don't mean a list of indented items, each one prefaced by a Roman numeral. (When have those been useful outside of school?)

By outline, I mean a list of all your story events, described in about a sentence apiece, and arranged (more or less) according to the order you envision them unfolding in your screenplay or novel.

With such an outline in hand, you won't get stranded. You'll know where your story is headed; you won't have to decide where to take it.

You'll always know what happens next.

Most likely, this prospect feels either comforting or confining to you.

If it's comforting, you're probably a "plotter," a writer who already outlines your stories in advance. You're sold on the benefits of outlining. You're well acquainted with its merits.

You're just looking for a better, more effective way to outline than the way you've got. This book might have what you need.

If this prospect feels confining to you, you're probably a "pantser," a writer who likes to write on the fly, by the seat of your pants, without an outline.

But if you're reading this writing guide right now, your current method isn't working anymore. It's starting to stress you out. It's not going to support your business goals.

Unlike plotters, you're not looking for a new way to outline. You're looking for a new way, period. Again, this book might have what you need.

When you know where your story is headed, you'll be able to write your rough draft with more confidence. That's a wonderful benefit, to be sure.

Even better, it's not the only one.

With an outline, you can easily identify thorny problem spots and gaping plot holes. Not like with a rough draft, where you have to slug through 100+ pages (in a screenplay) or 350+ pages (in a novel) to find them.

You're not looking for a needle in a haystack of words; you just have to comb through a few sentences. Much easier.

Much.

That's not all. Again, because you're dealing with a smaller volume of material, fixing problem spots and plot holes should require little to no time.

If you were working with a rough draft, you'd be looking at revising 500 words…5,000 words…and, in a worst-case scenario, even 50,000 words (ouch!).

Since you're only working with an outline, you just have to change a few words.

Maybe 50 or so.

This perk is invaluable. Once you become used to it, you'll probably become a hardcore outlining enthusiast.

That's the good news. Hold on to it, because I'm about to say something that you don't want to hear.

To enjoy the full range of benefits that outlining provides, you've got to outline your story more than once.

Yep. You heard me correctly.

You've got to generate multiple outlines, through a three-stage process I call *iterative outlining*.

Within each stage, your story will undergo several iterations. And, with each successive iteration, your story will improve. It will become stronger—and easier for you to write and edit it.

The stages look like this:

Stage 1: Generate a Starter Outline

A *starter outline* is like a starter home. You don't want to invest too much into it. You just want to generate raw material as quickly as you can, so you know what happens next in your story. This will boost your confidence.

Plus, with this raw material, you have something to shape and mold and improve upon during stages 2 and 3. If it turns out that a plot point you've come up with *doesn't work*, you've generated something to *work with*, and that will lead you to something that *does work*.

Incidentally, this principle is at the foundation of iterative outlining, and we'll come back to it often.

Stage 2: Articulate Your Intent

Humans are odd. We might be the only animal species whose behavior doesn't always match our intentions. This tendency manifests itself in a variety of ways.

With respect to storytelling, your starter outline may not, upon close inspection, actually tell the story you intended to tell.

Surprise!

For instance, while you intended your story to be a drama, when you examine your starter outline, it's turned into a comedy. Or, your story was supposed to be about John, but instead, it follows John's younger brother, Jimmy.

Results like these usually indicate one of two things: (1) you've come up with a new, perhaps superior, way to tell your story, or (2) your original approach is fine, but it's been occluded by irrelevant material.

Either way, you can't leave your story the way it is, in a jumble. If you don't take corrective measures, your ambivalence will be reflected in the final product. Your confusion will be transmitted to audiences. Instead of engaging with your story, they'll be too busy trying to figure out what it's about.

Thus, you have to sort out your intentions and commit to a unified vision. That's the focus of stage 2. During it, your starter outline will become progressively more consistent, ultimately evolving into an *intentional outline*.

Basically, you'll act as your own developmental editor or script consultant and iterate your way toward clarity—and a story with a clear and cohesive identity.

In some cases, to achieve clarity, you'll have to outline your story again (e.g. one time where John is clearly the hero; and another time, where Jimmy's clearly the hero). Then you can stack up your outlines side by side, compare them, and make a decision. John should be the hero, not Jimmy.

An inconvenient (and often overlooked) step, true. But it pays off in the long run. If you don't generate additional outlines, you'll waffle.

Should you stick to John? Should you forsake him for Jimmy?

Back and forth, back and forth, you'll go. Investing a little time now, up front, should help you avoid the mental strain of second-guessing yourself later.

Stage 3: Fix Problem Spots

This is where you'll assess your intentional outline and make changes as needed. You'll verify that your story is entertaining, and, at the same time, both credible and emotionally compelling.

This is where you'll work on problem spots like these:

- The plot is episodic, doesn't escalate well, or is loaded with contrivance.
- Opportunities to heighten audience emotion have been overlooked.
- Characters have been sacrificed for the sake of the plot (or other reasons).

- The subplots detract, rather than contribute toward, the main plot.
- The pacing is monotonous or sluggish (or perhaps, too frenetic).
- The cast is too large to keep audiences involved in what's happening.
- You've undermined your protagonist at the last minute.

As previously mentioned, having identified these problematic areas, you can fix them quite easily. All you have to do is rearrange a few words or sentences.

Snap! You're done.

Now you have a *working outline*. This is what you'll use during your writing sessions to speed through your rough draft.

Its name is inspired by the term *working title*, a temporary or provisional title given to a project in development in order to identify it until an official title is selected.

Like its namesake, a working outline isn't fixed in stone. You can deviate from it if you wish.

If you do, you'll be able to instantly see how these deviations will ripple throughout your story—and what changes you'll have to make as a consequence. This invariably makes revising your story a lot more manageable, and, in many cases, less time-consuming too.

There you have it. The three stages of iterative outlining. At first glance, this approach may seem rather unusual. But iterative outlining is actually standard practice. See, it mirrors writing advice that you've probably encountered before:

- say it (generate a starter outline)
- say what you mean (articulate your intent)
- say it well (fix problem spots)

All writing and revising follows this process in one way or another. While iterative outlining may seem like a lot of work, in truth, it condenses the whole ordeal. In the end, you more than make up for the time you invest up front.

By systematically progressing through each of the three stages, you'll be able to finish your rough draft with confidence and enviable efficiency. Not only that, your final product should be greatly improved as well.

But to get there, you need to complete stage 1 of iterative outlining.

You need a starter outline.

To make sure we're on the same page here, I want to emphasize that this writing guide, *Sizzling Story Outlines*, is about stage 1 and stage 1 only. It doesn't cover stages 2 and 3, which involve intentional and working outlines, respectively. If you're interested in stages 2 and 3, they are explored in depth in the other two books in the Iterative Outlining series: *Solid Story Compass* (stage 2) and *Sparkling Story Drafts* (stage 3).

Even though we're just covering stage 1 in *Sizzling Story Outlines*, you'll still learn a lot. Take a look:

Part I: How to Make Sure Your Story Idea Isn't a Waste of Time

When you get a seemingly great story idea, you probably like to "run with it." If you're a plotter, you're keen to dive into outlining. If you're a pantser, you want to jump into your rough draft.

Here's the thing: not all ideas are worth the time it takes to outline them, let alone write a first draft based on them.

No matter how you approach writing a screenplay or novel, you should take a moment to develop your story idea first, so it has the six components all compelling stories share.

This way, you can maximize its potential, making sure it has enough substance to sustain a full-length film or novel—and enough appeal to attract an audience to read (or watch) it.

Also, as a matter of practicality, this is the only way to generate an outline of value, one you can get mileage out of. You can't really plot your story in advance unless you first have some understanding of what it's about.

Part II: How to Build Your Story Structure

Even a great idea can collapse if it doesn't have solid structure to support it.

Technically, structure encompasses all of your scenes—and how you choose to arrange them. In this writing guide, though, we're working with a narrower definition, zooming onto an exclusive set of plot points. These are the load-bearing scenes, the critical turning points within your story.

When these are in place, you won't take forever to get your story "off the ground"; you won't blow the good stuff too soon; and you'll bring everything together in a satisfying conclusion.

In essence, when well executed, story structure ensures your screenplay or novel will become progressively more interesting as it goes along. You'll have a solid framework to support your heart-wrenching scenes or spine-tingling set pieces.

In addition, because you've figured out these structural signposts in advance, you won't be traversing in the dark, where you don't know what happens next, for very long.

You'll always have a bearing to head toward, a destination just around the corner.

Hence, you're unlikely to become so discouraged that you abandon your project altogether—the tragic result that frequently arises when you write blindly from FADE IN or Chapter 1.

Actually, this is also why starter outlines can be described as sizzling outlines. Not because they contain steamy love scenes or high-octane explosions (although they may).

With such an outline, when you sit down at your keyboard, you know you're not going to get lost along the way and abandon your rough draft in despair. You'll be fired up to write! That's why starter outlines sizzle.

Nevertheless, while beneficial, this isn't enough—not if you're a plotter. You need to know what happens next *all* of the time, not just some of the time. I don't have to convince you to move on, to Part III.

On the other hand, if you're a pantser, you might be content to stop here. This gives you a happy medium, the best of both worlds. Because you've already sorted out your story structure, you won't get stuck. You won't run out of steam.

At the same time, there is a lot of your story left to discover. You can stay close to your characters and "pants away" between each structural signpost.

You can still enjoy a sense of freedom when you write, and yet be secure in the knowledge that your story won't end in…well, a dead end. But if you'd like to enhance your efficiency, then I encourage you to continue on to…

Part III: How to Outline Your Story with a Method Backed by Scientific Research (Sort Of)

Here, I'll share with you a radical new outlining method that will help you take your characters from one structural signpost to the next. With this method, you'll be able to plot out your entire story in as little as 2 hours.

Even better, this method incorporates a simple technique Stanford researchers have concluded can make you 60% more creative (on average).

Plus, I'll show you five easy ways to make this outlining method even more effective. (Number four is pretty intriguing, if I do say so myself.)

Having implemented this radical outlining method, you will have a complete starter outline, a full list of all the plot points in your story. So, when you sit down to write, you won't have to think about what happens next.

You'll know.

You can finish your rough draft without freaking out.

Can you hear that?

It's the sound of you hammering out words on your keyboard, like you're Thor.

Nice.

Take It Easy—Step by Step

Writing a screenplay or novel is a daunting task. However, it becomes far more manageable if it's broken down into smaller action steps.

This writing guide does that. Where appropriate, each chapter ends with simple action steps that, together, form a practical, systematic way to map out your story.

Below is a sampling of what you will accomplish by following these steps:

- Your protagonist's goal will have the attributes necessary to prevent audience attention from drifting away.
- Although completely different on the surface, *Inception* and *Night at the Museum* share a feature that ensured audiences would be emotionally invested in these films; your story will share it, too.
- You'll make your story idea more ironic, and hence, more commercial.

- Using a simple template, you'll produce a one-sentence summary of your story. (This will help you write and market it.)
- You'll figure out your first-act break and inciting incident in 10 minutes (probably less).
- You'll crack the middle of your story (including the midpoint and the end of Act Two), so that writing it will be less of a stress fest.
- You'll take measures to prevent your screenplay or novel from wimping out during the climax.
- You'll have a list of all the plot points in your story, ultimately enabling you to write a better story, faster (no fancy software required).

Sounds good, right?

But before we continue, you should be aware of the following:

(1) Unless otherwise indicated, the tips in this book apply equally to screenplays and novels.

Despite this, I primarily use film examples to illustrate my points. That's because movies are more universal.

Chances are greater that you've watched, rather than read, *Mrs. Doubtfire*. (Honestly, did you know the film was based on a book? I didn't learn that until recently!)

On paper, the titles of films adapted from novels (or a TV series) appear the same as novel (or TV) titles. Customarily, all are indicated via italics. But since I mainly rely on film examples, unless otherwise noted, it's safe to assume I'm referencing the film version only.

(2) There are a ton of examples in this writing guide…which means there are some spoilers too.

A few of these examples may've cropped up on my website, scribemeetsworld.com, or in other writing guides I've authored.

(3) I analyze stories using three-act structure. You might not like using three-act structure. That's cool. You can still benefit from this writing guide.

Where appropriate, just replace Act One with "the beginning," Act Two with "the middle," and Act Three with "the end" of your story. This way, you'll be able to make use of all the practical advice in this book without any quibbling over structure.

(4) As described earlier, stage 1 of iterative outlining consists of three parts. Each focuses on a different aspect of developing your story. To facilitate your understanding, I use a different metaphor to explain each part. Basically, this is a quick heads-up: the metaphors will change throughout this book!

(5) As previously mentioned, most chapters end with a set of action steps. For your convenience, a master list with pared-down descriptions of each step can be found at the end of this book, in chapter 20.

Whether you're a plotter or a pantser, I encourage you to follow all the action steps, in sequence, at least once. Afterward, you can adapt this method to your taste, using what appeals to you and discarding the rest.

(6) Finally, for the sake of simplicity, I tend to stick to masculine nouns and pronouns.

Okay, that's all.

Are you ready to generate the starter outline that will boost your confidence, and ultimately, reduce your revision time?

Let's go!

- PART I -

HOW TO MAKE SURE YOUR STORY IDEA ISN'T A WASTE OF TIME, A.K.A. POPPING THE STORY KERNEL

DOES THIS SOUND FAMILIAR?

All of a sudden, as you're driving to work, dropping off your kids at school, or drifting off to sleep, a miracle occurs.

Out of the blue, you're struck by a burst of inspiration. You discover an idea that appears rife with potential. It could yield an amazing screenplay or novel.

Naturally, when this happens, all you want to do is take this idea and run with it, right?

Completely understandable.

With writing often compared to painful things—pulling teeth, spilling blood, giving birth—no wonder you want to capitalize on the moment, and begin the process when you're filled with enthusiasm.

While yielding to this inclination is understandable, unfortunately, it can also be self-defeating.

When you rush to outline a story or write a rough draft, without thoroughly scrutinizing your idea, it's possible that you could produce a gripping tale that will enthrall audiences and solidify your writing career.

Possible, but not likely.

More often than not, one of two things will happen. About a third of the way into your story, you'll hit a wall. You won't finish it.

Not because you lack talent or willpower, but because your story idea is fundamentally flawed. It doesn't have enough substance, or meat, to it; it can't support a full-length screenplay or novel.

Alternatively, when you take your idea and run with it, you may hit a few blocks, but not enough to derail you completely. You do produce a full-length final draft.

Trouble is, no one wants to read it.

Again, your idea is fundamentally flawed. Even if executed perfectly, it simply isn't interesting enough to capture anyone's attention.

Either outcome amounts to a lot of heartache—and wasted hours—for you.

Happily, it's very easy to protect yourself from this anguish. All you need to do is resist the urge to run with your idea. Instead, take a little time to develop it first.

This is what I call *popping the story kernel*. Doing so will help you assess whether your idea is worthwhile to pursue, so you don't waste your time writing thousands of words that go nowhere. For this reason, it's a step you should take whether or not you embrace iterative outlining (or, for that matter, whether you even engage in outlining at all).

As a practical issue (assuming you do embrace iterative outlining), popping the story kernel is the only way to generate a starter outline of value, one you can actually get mileage out of. You can't really plot your story in advance unless you first have some understanding of what it's about.

In practice, popping the story kernel entails teasing out six components that are shared by all compelling stories, components that you want to have in place before you devote weeks, months—perhaps a year or more—to your rough draft.

Here they are:

- protagonist
- goal
- antagonist
- stakes
- genre
- hook

We'll explore each of these in the following chapters. But before we begin, a quick disclaimer: you'll notice that theme is missing from this list.

Don't get me wrong. Theme is important and powerful. More than anything else, it's instrumental in giving your story the kind of longevity that lasts even beyond your lifetime. In fact, as you'll see in chapter 2, you may derive your protagonist and his goal from your story's theme.

Even so, in order to assess whether your idea is compelling enough to first attract—and then captivate a decent-sized audience—it's not imperative to know the theme of your story beforehand.

With this disclaimer out of the way, let's get poppin'!

- chapter one -

GETTING STARTED VIA THE STORY KERNEL

BEFORE YOU CAN POP YOUR STORY KERNEL, YOU'VE got to isolate it. To do that, it helps to understand what it is. So let's get back to basics.

Typically, when you're struck by a burst of inspiration, a lot of bits and pieces come with it. I call these *story seeds*. They can be an unusual circumstance, a character name or trait, a particular image, a killer action stunt, or various lines of dialogue.

Everything and anything.

Of these seeds, one tends to encompass the others. You sense its importance immediately. This is the story kernel. It usually involves one of three things:

- an intriguing situation (a bomb is on a bus, and it will explode if the bus goes below 50 mph, as in *Speed*)

- a character with protagonist potential (a reclusive man is so obsessive-compulsive, he uses a fresh bar of soap every time he washes his hands, as in *As Good As It Gets*)
- a theme that you relate to (you want to explore what it means to be a winner, as in *Little Miss Sunshine*)

To build a full-fledged outline, you'll expand upon this story kernel—and only the story kernel.

That's it.

The remaining story seeds should be set aside.

Right now, you might be recoiling at this suggestion. Ignore your awesome riff on *Star Wars*? The scene where the hero spills his heart out to the heroine? The cool stunt with the decoy moving van?

I can understand your reluctance. It's easy to become attached to story seeds because you associate them with good times, when your ideas flowed effortlessly, when there wasn't such a thing as a blank page because you were furiously—joyously—filling it up with possibilities.

Plus, since story seeds are part and parcel of your original burst of inspiration, it seems almost wrong to omit them.

But you have to let go.

See, as wonderful as that burst of inspiration is, it only gives you an inkling of what your story is going to be like. You still don't know what kind of story you're trying to tell.

Not yet, not without further exploration.

Even if you think you do, at this stage, you probably don't. Over the course of outlining your story, it's going to change, grow, evolve. It's not going to be quite the same beast you originally conceived of. Consequently, your original story seeds may no longer be right for your screenplay or novel.

Just because they were there, at the beginning, when you first launched your project, doesn't automatically mean they should stay. They have to earn their keep.

If you give them automatic admittance, and try to shoehorn them into your outline as you're building it, you'll wind up with an incoherent, uneven story that pleases no one.

Once you've finished your outline, however, it's a different matter altogether. Enough time has passed for you to gain some distance and overcome your initial attachment to your story seeds.

You'll have a clearer understanding of what kind of story you want to tell, and you'll be in a better position to evaluate whether your story seeds should be incorporated into your draft, and how to accomplish this without undue contrivance.

When you conduct your assessment, you'll probably discover that you've already included a few story seeds in your outline because they came to you, unbidden, during the development process (which, you'll notice, is a lot different than forcefully crowbarring them in).

With other story seeds, you'll realize that they don't belong in your story. At least, not directly.

Their real value lies in a more indirect application: problem solving.

Oftentimes, when you've identified problem spots in your outline (especially in the third act), returning to your story seeds will initiate a brainstorming session that will lead you to the perfect solution.

The basic takeaway here is this: the story seeds produced by your initial burst of inspiration may not belong in your story at all. But in crunch times, re-examining them can lead you to what *does* belong, which is why they're a real lifesaver and worth holding on to.

Actually, this principle—of using old possibilities to generate new, more viable ones—is at the heart of iterative outlining. It will crop up several times throughout this book!

ACTION STEP(S)

(1) Isolate your story kernel.

When you're struck by a burst of inspiration, jot down all of the ideas that ensue. Isolate the story kernel—situation, character, or theme—and then put away your remaining story seeds. Don't refer to them again until you've finished your outline.

If you're working from a preexisting (perhaps abandoned) project, first give yourself permission to start fresh, with a clean slate. A simple step, but a critical one.

Then, isolate the story kernel. Depending on how much work

you've already done, you might have all three types: situation, character, and theme. That's fine. Treat *everything else* as part of your "seed bank."

- chapter two -

SHAPING AUDIENCE EXPERIENCE VIA SMART GOALS AND THE PROTAGONIST

ALL RIGHT, YOU HAVE YOUR STORY KERNEL. NOW it's time to connect it to a clear, overarching goal.

This is not a "sexy" task, like creating character backstories or blocking out fight scenes.

You may consider it grunt work, especially if you're dazzled by the cleverness, inventiveness, or resonance of your story kernel. (The bus can't go below 50 mph! My protagonist unwraps a new bar of soap every time he washes his hands. Every time!)

But you can't get sidetracked by your story kernel. You can't yield to the temptation of taking your idea and running with it. As mundane as the task may feel, you must first establish a goal for your protagonist. Why?

Three reasons, mainly.

First, the actions your protagonist takes to achieve his goal will form the building blocks of your plot, and hence, determine a significant portion of its structure. Without a clear protagonist goal, the plot and structure of your story are unlikely to be sound. Your screenplay or novel will lack narrative drive, which brings me to reason #2.

When your protagonist pursues his goal with single-minded intensity, audience attention is, likewise, likely to remain focused. Conversely, if your protagonist pursues vague or multiple goals, audience attention is likely to dissipate…until it vanishes altogether. Having lost interest, audiences will abandon your story and pick up another screenplay or novel in their TBR pile.

Finally, and perhaps most important, a well-chosen goal gives audiences something to root for. You can't say the same for a situation (as intriguing as it seems), an aimless character (as interesting as he is), or theme (no matter how evocative). To sum it up, in conjunction with stakes and likeability, your protagonist's goal determines how emotionally invested audiences are going to be.

We'll briefly discuss stakes later on, in chapter 4. But for now, let's keep our eyes on one particular prize: your protagonist's goal.

Not every goal will produce the three benefits we just talked about. To ensure that yours has the potential to yield such benefits, consider borrowing a technique from project management.

Make your goal a SMART one.

Each letter of the acronym stands for an attribute which, having been established beforehand, makes it more likely that an employee (or a team of them) will accomplish the goal in the first place.

If we adapt this technique for our purposes, a SMART goal for your protagonist would be:

S – Specific (it's concrete, not amorphous or abstract)

M – Measureable (it has a clear indicator of success or failure)

A – Actionable (even a brief description immediately conjures up a few of the action steps needed to accomplish it)

R – Realistic (it's credible for *your* protagonist to achieve it)

T – Time-bound (it must be accomplished by a certain deadline)

More details on creating a SMART goal for your protagonist—as well as on creating the protagonist himself—can be found in the next section!

Reverse Engineering SMART Goals

Whew. That was a lot to digest in a short period of time.

If you're feeling a bit lost, don't worry. In this section, we'll examine how to reverse engineer a SMART goal from each type of story kernel:

- situation
- character
- theme

By the time we're through, you should be able to choose a suitable SMART goal for your protagonist in no time!

Reverse Engineering from Situation

Often, with a situation-based story kernel, a SMART goal is implied by the situation you came up with in action step #1.

Returning to *Speed*, the presence of the bomb automatically lends itself to a SMART goal: someone (presumably the hero) must stop the bomb from detonating.

Not a lot of detail, sure, but that's all you need because this goal has all the attributes you're looking for. It's:

- specific (self-explanatory, I think)
- measurable (either the bomb goes off or it doesn't)
- actionable (at the very least, the hero will have to board the bus, examine the bomb, and figure out who's responsible)
- realistic (if the hero is physically fit and has experience with explosives, it's believable he could take on this mission)
- time-bound (assuming the hero can keep the bus going above 50 mph, the deadline is dictated by the amount of fuel in the bus's tank)

As you can see, when you reverse engineer a SMART goal from an intriguing situation, in the process, you'll also figure out the protagonist of your story (if you didn't know that already). You might not know much about him at this point, but you know enough to figure out the rest as you go along.

I chose *Speed* as an example not just because it's an easy one to understand but also because it illustrates an important point about action movies and thrillers. Frequently, the hero's goal is *to stop* the antagonist's plans.

Thus, it can be helpful to first define the *antagonist's goal* (SMARTly, naturally), and then direct your attention onto your hero, whose own SMART goal, to spell it out, would simply be to stop the antagonist's SMART goal.

Let's look at another example, this time from a romantic comedy. In *What Women Want*, a male chauvinist suddenly develops the ability to hear women's thoughts. It's an intriguing situation which, similar to *Speed*, also predefines the protagonist. But, unlike *Speed*, it doesn't automatically imply a clear, overarching goal.

This is liable to get amateurs into all sorts of trouble, as they get caught up in the fun antics that could arise from this situation… and neglect to give their protagonist a SMART goal.

When they run out of antics, they won't know how to advance their story forward, and the plot will come to a standstill. Sadly, their exciting concept won't seem so exciting anymore. Fortunately, their concept can be salvaged once they give their protagonist clear direction via a goal.

Notice that in *What Women Want*, the protagonist's situation is paired with a SMART goal. Nick wants to use his newfound ability to steal back the promotion he had been eyeing from the woman who got it instead of him. So, when the film is done showing how Nick reacts to his magical windfall (lots of fun, but it can't last forever), it still has somewhere to go and new territory to mine.

Reverse Engineering from Character

Similar to situation-based story kernels, character-based kernels can automatically imply a SMART goal.

For instance, after a burst of inspiration strikes, you may come up with a character you'd like to write about and whom others would love to read about. A sassy female bounty hunter, like Janet Evanovich's Stephanie Plum, for instance.

You have the protagonist; now she just needs a goal. In this example, her profession suggests one right off the bat: apprehend a bail jumper.

Again, I want to draw your attention to the level of specificity here. We don't know anything else about the bail jumper, so in one sense, this goal is generic.

Yet, it's specific enough to be measurable (the protagonist either catches him or she doesn't) and actionable (staking out the bail jumper's home, interviewing his friends and family, and using the resulting leads to track him down at his current hidey-hole are a few steps that immediately come to mind).

That's the minimum level of specificity you're aiming for. Of course, if your imagination provides you with more details, that's excellent, but they're not a necessity at this stage of the game.

Granted, this goal needs some refinement (in the realistic and time-bound departments), but we can delay these items for now. We've gotten specific enough—SMART enough—to give our story strong narrative drive.

Designing a SMART goal is especially important in character-driven stories, where your protagonist has to overcome some tragedy from the past (often referred to as a *ghost*) or a deep-rooted flaw.

Although overcoming the past and transforming into a better person are worthwhile goals—and, in fact, may be the point of your story—they're too vague to build your entire infrastructure upon.

Instead, to give your story focus, you need to drill deeper, and think of a *specific, concrete* objective whose pursuit will challenge your protagonist to change.

Say, for example, you became fascinated with the JFK assassination, particularly its effect on the Secret Service agents who failed to protect the president. What are their lives like now? This question leads you to a character-based story kernel: a Secret Service agent haunted by the assassination of JFK.

To derive a SMART goal from this kernel, your thought process might look something like this:

- to redeem himself (no good; it's too vague)
- to redeem himself for failing to protect JFK (still no dice; it's more specific, but lacks the kind of specificity you're looking for)
- to redeem himself for past failure by stopping an assassination attempt in the present (bingo, you got it!)

As you probably realize, this is the plot of *In the Line of Fire*, starring Clint Eastwood. But it didn't have to be. In theory, Eastwood's character could pursue a different kind of goal, but one that would incubate his redemption just as well.

For the sake of discussion, we could transplant Eastwood's Secret Service hero into another one of his films, *Gran Torino*. In order to redeem himself for failing to save the life of JFK in the past, an aging Secret Service agent (while fulfilling his current job duties) tries to rescue a Vietnamese teenager from the clutches of a local gang in the present.

Do you see how giving your protagonist a goal that's too vague (i.e. to redeem himself) can produce a story that's devoid of cohesion?

In this hypothetical, one minute the hero would be trying to rescue the current president, and in the next, his immigrant neighbor. Taking this example even further, the hero may try to rescue yet another character.

At first glance, this combination may seem cohesive because each of our hero's "rescue missions" falls under the global umbrella of seeking redemption.

But it isn't.

While each rescue mission is linked via character arc (from feeling guilty to being redeemed), they aren't linked via plot. There's no cause-and-effect relationship between them.

The end product won't be a story with strong narrative drive, clear focus, and unified structure. It'll be a collection of episodic vignettes.

There's a market for these kinds of stories, sure, but it's limited. And if you're reading this book, I assume that's not your target audience. Your audience is looking for something far less meandering.

Admittedly, the Clint Eastwood films I used as examples take this idea to the extreme. It's unlikely for a writer to combine the president's re-election campaign from *Fire* with the neighborhood crime of *Gran Torino*, without ever realizing that his story has gone off the rails.

Still, this kind of thing happens all the time. If you're writing a character-driven story, be especially on your guard.

Give your story the focus necessary to sustain audience interest.

Work from a SMART goal, not from your protagonist's ghost, flaws, or quirks.

Say, for instance, that your character-based story kernel results in a protagonist who uses a fresh bar of soap every time he washes his hands (Melvin Udall, *As Good As It Gets*) or who throws a paperback copy of *A Farewell to Arms* out of a closed window—thereby breaking the glass—because the novel's ending is too depressing (Pat Solitano, *Silver Linings Playbook*).

Although such a protagonist is intriguing, and is likely to fascinate audiences, don't become so enamored by him that you stop there. Quirky actions, even a whole series of them, can't sustain audience interest over the long haul. Once the novelty wears off, audience attention will quickly dissipate.

That is, unless you give your quirky protagonist a SMART goal to pursue.

In both *As Good As It Gets* and *Silver Linings Playbook*, the goal involves pursuit of a romantic relationship. Melvin, with a local waitress; Pat, with his estranged wife.

Notice how this goal affects audience response. It inspires curiosity (audiences wonder how such flawed protagonists will achieve their respective goals) and invokes emotional involvement (assuming audiences have bonded with the protagonists, audiences will also root for the two men to accomplish their goals).

Reverse Engineering from Theme

Theme is tricky.

Unlike situation-based story kernels (which often come with, or quickly lead to, a clear goal and/or protagonist) and character-based kernels (which basically give you a protagonist), with a theme-based kernel, you have to create both a goal and a protagonist from scratch.

There are other drawbacks, too. When you reverse engineer from theme, it's possible for you to put the cart (the theme) before the horse (the plot). Your final draft might be more of a message than a story.

In addition, your story runs the risk of being episodic, with multiple events connecting via theme but not via plot. (As aforementioned, character-driven stories with a vague protagonist goal are plagued by a similar pitfall.)

That said, reverse engineering from theme is doable. *Little Miss Sunshine* provides us with a fine example. According to *Wikipedia* (citing FORA.tv), the genesis of the script came from an unlikely source—a comment made by Arnold Schwarzenegger. "If there's one thing in this world I hate, it's losers. I despise them." [1]

Screenwriter Michael Arndt wanted to "lampoon" this way of thinking. "I wanted to…attack that idea that in life you're going up or you're going down."

As you can see, this theme is pretty amorphous. What does it mean to go up or down?

What does that *look* like?

Fortunately, Arndt quickly connected this vague idea to something more concrete: a child beauty pageant. In his own words, "It's the epitome of the ultimate stupid meaningless competition people put themselves through."

And from this concrete setting, it's a piece of cake to reverse engineer a SMART goal: to win a child beauty pageant.

Unlike the general idea of going up, even without further detail, it's specific enough to produce an image of what it looks like. It's also specific enough to yield a potential protagonist: the young girl who must participate in the pageant.

To be thorough, let's see how this goal fulfills the other SMART requirements. Winning the pageant is measurable. Either the young girl is crowned Little Miss Sunshine, or she isn't. Clear action steps come to mind: preparing a talent routine, traveling to the pageant, and taking the stage, for instance. It's time-bound too, with a deadline dictated by pageant regulations.

So, we've got the S, the M, the A, and the T. What about the R? Is this goal realistic?

Well…no, actually. Not for the protagonist Arndt has chosen. She is plain and chubby, not traditional beauty-queen material.

However, she is brimming with naïveté and fervent enthusiasm. While it's not realistic for her to win, it's believable that she would attempt to. This works, fittingly enough, due to theme. The whole point of Arndt's story is that going up doesn't necessarily mean winning, but at least having the courage to try.

If your protagonist, unlike *Sunshine*'s, does accomplish his goal—even though, at the outset, it's not believable he would—you've got to expend more effort to make his eventual success credible.

We'll cover some specific techniques in the next chapter. For now, just recognize that out of all the SMART-goal attributes, *realistic* is the most flexible, often taking on different meanings depending on genre and theme.

Can a Protagonist Change His SMART Goal?

Yes—but it's a risky move.

Your story can feel disjointed, as if you've strung together two separate plots that don't really belong together, despite sharing the same protagonist.

Not only that, your final product will probably come across as underdeveloped. See, by switching SMART goals midway through your story, you don't have to explore—in depth—the trials of accomplishing a single goal.

Instead, you can explore these trials superficially, before your protagonist moves on to a new target, which will, more than likely, receive equally superficial treatment.

If you're tempted to switch your protagonist's goal, be honest with yourself. Is this going to change the direction of your story in a way that audiences will embrace with enthusiasm? Or is this just a way for you to avoid the challenges that come with sustaining an idea for over a 100 pages (in a screenplay) or 350 pages (in a novel)?

There is one type of story where goal switches are not only successful, but par for course: "want vs. need" stories. The protagonist pursues something (the want), but in order to be truly happy, he must pursue something else (the need)—necessitating a goal switch.

If you know you're writing a want-vs.-need story, these observations may be helpful:

- Both the protagonist's want and his need should be defined SMARTly.
- Frequently, the need will be defined as the obtainment of a romantic relationship.
- If the protagonist must give up his want in order to obtain his need, he usually does so as part of the climax.
- In some cases, by being willing to give up the want for the sake of the need, the protagonist is able to have both.

- The want-vs.-need pattern is often found in romances where the hero and heroine need each other but initially pursue something else (like a promotion or the wrong guy or girl). Give this pursuit its proper due and define it carefully. Functioning like a clothesline for the burgeoning romance to hang off of, it will drive your plot forward and gird its structure.

ACTION STEP(S)

(2) Design your SMART goal, which will anchor the plot of your story, as well as the protagonist who will pursue it.

Focus on making the goal specific, measurable, and actionable. For the moment, don't stress over making it realistic and time-bound. (But if these come to you anyway, great!)

If it helps, start with your antagonist's goal, and then work backward to determine your protagonist's goal.

Speaking of the protagonist, if you haven't already, it's time to come up with one. What kind of person is necessitated by the SMART goal you've devised and the genre you've chosen? (By the way, more details on genre are around the corner, in chapter 5.)

Remember, you don't need to have all the details. "To catch a bail jumper" (without knowing anything about the bail jumper) works just fine as a SMART goal. "Someone who has experience with explosives" will suffice as a description of your protagonist. There'll be opportunities to refine both of these elements later on.

However, there's a difference between not having all the details and being too vague. "To get his life in order" doesn't cut it as a SMART goal. But "to complete all 12 steps in the Alcoholics Anonymous program" does make the grade.

Likewise, "to go on a dangerous mission" shouldn't be the goal of your action hero. On the other hand, "to retrieve a priceless diamond from the arms dealer who inadvertently acquired it" works very nicely.

A quick note on theme: if you started with a theme-based story kernel and are concerned about letting theme overtake your story, consider adding the theme to your seed bank.

That is, add it to the list of story seeds generated in action step #1…and set it aside. Develop your story as if the theme doesn't exist.

Once you've finished your starter outline, you can see how well your story expresses the theme you intended it to convey.

Please note, this is a suggestion only. Ignore it if it gives you the heebie-jeebies. Oh, if you didn't start with a theme-based story kernel, examining your completed starter outline can help you find a suitable theme for your story.

- chapter three -

CONJURING CONFLICT TO ENTERTAIN AUDIENCES VIA THE ANTAGONIST

IT AIN'T EASY BEING A PROTAGONIST.

It can't be.

Not when conflict is necessary to keep audiences interested in a story.

And now, it's time to identify a major source of this conflict: the antagonist.

Who's going to challenge your protagonist's pursuit of his SMART goal?

More than one person may fit the bill, but we're focusing on the "top dog" here, the individual with the most power, intelligence, and charisma; the one who *repeatedly* comes in between your protagonist and his goal.

Notice two things. I said *antagonist*, not *villain*. True, many great antagonists are villains, but antagonists come in various shapes and sizes. They may be:

- nemeses (equally driven as villains, but not evil)
- rivals (a special kind of nemesis who competes with the protagonist for the same goal)
- amorous opponents (two characters who "battle" to secure love or affection from each other)

I also said *person*, not *flaw*. A flaw doesn't cut it as an antagonist, at least not by itself. Your antagonist must arise from an external source.

In a screenplay, this is critical because a camera can't perceive thoughts. To tell your story, you're limited to what can be seen or heard. An internal battle, wherein your protagonist's flaw vies for dominance, doesn't qualify. (Okay. Voiceover enables you to reveal a character's thoughts, but it's often a crutch and should be used sparingly, if at all.)

In a novel, through interior monologue, you can go wild with your protagonist's thoughts. For a book lover, being privy to these thoughts is one of the greatest attractions of reading—up to a point.

A balance must be struck.

By integrating an external antagonist into your story from the get-go, you ensure that your protagonist won't sit around all day, thinking up a storm. No matter how fascinating his internal struggle or thoughts are, this is going to get old.

Fast.

There's another reason not to rely on a flaw as your story's antagonist, and this reason applies to both screenplays and novels. At its heart, the climax is the final confrontation between the protagonist and his antagonist.

Without a visible antagonist, the climax of your story isn't going to have much thunder.

What is your protagonist going to do?

Tell his flaw to take a hike?

I don't think so.

But, at the climax, in order to demonstrate his transformation into a less self-centered human being, he can doggedly interrogate the villain in court (*A Few Good Men*); chase down a friend to prevent him from committing social suicide (*About a Boy*); or cede his promotion to a rival, who also happens to be his love interest (*What Women Want*).

Speaking of the climax, this is a good opportunity to revisit the R in our SMART acronym. Why is it realistic for your protagonist (assuming victory) to achieve his goal at your story's end?

Maybe your protagonist's background makes it believable that he can handle himself well at the climax. If you already know that your protagonist must be someone who (a) is physically fit and (b) has experience with explosives (as is the case with *Speed*), now's the time to weed through credible possibilities and specify his current (or past) profession and hobbies that would gain him such expertise.

In other cases, it's not so clear-cut. If your protagonist starts out as an underdog or a naïf or a bungler—i.e. the most unlikely candidate to succeed—you have to expend more effort to believably bring about his climactic success.

To get you brainstorming, here are a few possibilities to consider (you may need to combine a few of these to reach the requisite level of credibility):

- A mentor helps the protagonist develop the skills that the protagonist initially lacks.
- The time frame is long enough for the protagonist to develop new skills (not necessarily with a mentor).
- The protagonist's journey brings to the surface a character trait (like courage or selflessness) the protagonist suppressed or didn't think he had.
- By himself, the protagonist wouldn't be able to handle the antagonist. Happily, the protagonist is paired with another character who possesses a complementary skill set.
- A prophecy or vision predicts the protagonist will succeed.
- Another character has faith in the protagonist's abilities.
- Another character makes a sacrifice that gains the protagonist a critical advantage.

ACTION STEP(S)

(3a) Create the main antagonist of your story.

What does he want? (You may've already answered this question in action step #2.)

What is his background? What is his profession? How does he compare to the protagonist in terms of combat training (action movie) or temperament (romance)?

Set the bar high.

When your antagonist is amazing, your protagonist is forced to rise to the occasion—netting you a higher-quality story.

(3b) Refine your protagonist accordingly.

What kind of person can go head-to-head with the antagonist you created in action step #3a? What physical, emotional, and psychological traits must he possess?

(4) Tackle your credibility strategy.

Choose a profession for your protagonist or build a backstory for him that would, from your story's outset, make it believable for him to succeed.

Alternatively, think about why your protagonist—despite his apparent shortcomings—was chosen for this mission and how he'll eventually best the villain (in an action movie) or why his amorous opponent would overcome her initial resistance toward him (in a romance).

Notice there's a feedback loop of sorts between your antagonist and protagonist. When you change a feature of your protagonist, you may go back and tweak the backstory of your antagonist. And then, in light of the new information you've just discovered about your antagonist, you'll further modify your protagonist.

Repeat this cycle until you're satisfied with the results.

(5) Create an additional antagonist, if necessary.

Your story may involve other antagonists too, like henchmen. But you don't need to create these second-tier antagonists in advance, not with the outlining method I'm going to describe in Part III. (But if ideas for such characters come to you now, by all means, jot them down!)

That said, it is possible that your concept warrants creating two antagonists in advance. If you're writing a want-vs.-need story, for instance. In action step #3a, you created the antagonist who'll stand in the way of your protagonist's want. Now, create the antagonist who'll stand in the way of your protagonist's need.

Here's another situation where you'll probably need to create two antagonists now: your plot is driven by a love triangle. For example, in *This Means War*, two spies fall in love with the same girl. From the point of view of one spy, the other is a rival (antagonist #1), while the girl is his amorous opponent (antagonist #2).

If you're writing a romance that (a) isn't driven by a love triangle (either it's absent altogether, or if present, it isn't—like *This Means War*—the story's central focus) and (b) involves at least one protagonist who's actively pursuing something besides love, then again, you'll also have to create two antagonists.

If this description seems confusing, the following example, with a hypothetical heroine, should help clarify. Although she's not initially seeking love, this heroine will eventually have to pursue a romantic relationship with the hero. Otherwise the story wouldn't be a romance. As her amorous opponent, he's antagonist #1.

By the same token, since the heroine isn't, at first, pursuing love, she has to pursue something else, something SMART. Otherwise the story would lack structural integrity. The character who stands between the heroine and this goal is antagonist #2.

If these conditions describe your romance, don't invest too much energy into this action step. Wait until you've reached chapter 6. There, I'll show you a simple trick you can use with antagonists #1 and #2 to make your story more ironic, and hence, more commercial.

- chapter four -

GIVING AUDIENCES A REASON TO CARE ABOUT YOUR STORY VIA THE STAKES

*I*N ORDER TO.

If there were a list of words or phrases that are crucial to writing a great story, this one would be in my top three.

Earlier on, we discussed how your protagonist's goal gives audiences something to root for. That is only part of the picture. To root for your protagonist, audiences must also know the stakes, i.e. the negative consequences of failing to achieve this goal.

With great stakes, audiences will be screaming themselves hoarse as they cheer on your protagonist; with mediocre or nonexistent stakes, they'll be halfheartedly clapping, assuming they muster up any enthusiasm at all.

That's why you must hitch your protagonist's goal to the phrase *in order to*.

By attaching stakes to your protagonist's goal, you give audiences a reason to care about it, a reason to stick around and see what happens next.

Consider the blockbuster films *Inception* and *Night at the Museum*. In *Inception*, Cobb, who normally infiltrates people's dreams to extract intel from them, must plant information instead. In *Night at the Museum*, Larry becomes a security guard at a museum where the exhibits come to life at night.

I think we can both agree these films ace the hook department. (We'll cover hooks in greater detail in chapter 6. For now, let's just say that a hook is an audience attractor.)

While these hooks are intriguing enough to garner audience interest, they can't sustain it. Alone, these hooks couldn't make these films blockbusters.

Here's why: as your story progresses, your protagonist should encounter increasingly more difficult obstacles. (If he doesn't, your story will lack conflict and escalation, and will fail for different reasons.)

Logically, in the face of such overwhelming obstacles, your protagonist should probably *stop* pursuing his goal. When he doesn't, audiences will quickly conclude that he's only persevering for the sake of their amusement. This taints their experience, making it feel contrived, trivial, and pointless.

As a result, they'll disengage from your story—unless, that is, you give them a reason not to.

When your protagonist has a compelling motivation to stay in the game, this potential source of audience disengagement is removed. Other factors being equal, audiences should happily stick around to see what happens. Better still, they'll be even more emotionally invested in what they experience.

Returning to *Inception* and *Night at the Museum*, both films build their stakes by mining the powerful resonance of the relationship between a father and his children.

Why must Cobb infiltrate multiple dream levels?

In order to regain access to his children and "see their faces" again.

Why must Larry continue to deal with the unruly museum exhibits?

In order to keep his job, and thus, prevent his son from thinking that his dad (i.e. Larry) is a loser.

Both of these are great stakes. They are motivations audiences can understand, get onboard with, and root for.

At this point, you might be wondering about likeability. If audiences care about your protagonist, won't they automatically care about what happens in your story?

Sure—but there's a limit.

Generally speaking, it's defined by genre and the kinds of risks your protagonist must take to succeed.

In a romance, for instance, the future happiness of the hero and heroine may be the only thing at stake. In this case, likeability is critical. Audiences will care about a potentially unhappy future only to the extent they like the protagonists.

But in other kinds of stories, likeability alone cannot sustain audience involvement. In *Night at the Museum*, as much as audiences like or feel sorry for Larry, without stakes, they're still going to wonder why he doesn't just quit his awful job. (In fact, at one point in the movie, he does, but the stakes reel him back in.)

In *Inception*, Cobb is not that likeable at all. Nevertheless, the poignancy of the stakes compels audiences to care about the story's outcome. Even if, hypothetically speaking, Cobb were more of a likeable guy, it still wouldn't matter. Without stakes, audiences are going to question why Cobb would want to infiltrate three dream levels when doing so could cost him his sanity.

By the way, if you want to know how to craft emotionally compelling stakes that keep readers glued to your pages or how to raise the stakes (even when they're already high to begin with), check out my writing guide *Story Stakes*.

ACTION STEP(S)

(6) Determine your story stakes.

Hitch your protagonist's SMART goal from action step #2 to the phrase *in order to*.

For example, why must FBI Agent Sean Archer undergo a facial transplant and take on the visage of the criminal mastermind who killed Archer's own son (*Face/Off*)?

In order to stop a "biblical" plague from destroying L.A.

Why must Rocky survive 15 rounds against Apollo Creed (*Rocky*)?

In order to prove that he isn't a bum.

A quick heads-up, just for romance writers: if you're writing a romance where the protagonist isn't, at first, pursuing love (but a different SMART goal), figure out the stakes attached to this SMART goal now.

If the romance puts these stakes in jeopardy, you must find a credible way to reconcile the two. You don't have to do this now, but you will have to address it eventually.

- chapter five -

ATTRACTING AUDIENCES VIA GENRE

WHY DO PEOPLE READ BOOKS AND WATCH MOVIES?

They want to be entertained, of course.

But a random story—even if it's well told—won't suffice.

That's because audiences don't just want a good story. (That's a given.)

For the most part, audiences want something more specific. *They want a good story that provides them with a particular kind of emotional experience.*

This is what genre is all about.

It's a categorization system that tells audiences, *This book or this movie has the emotional experience you're looking for. This story has what you* want.

If audiences want to experience the thrill of falling in love, only a romance will satisfy. If they want to be spooked, the horror genre is where they'll look; if they want to be amused, a comedy will be just the ticket.

If they want a kinetic, fast-paced experience with car chases and explosions, they'll seek out stories in the action and thriller genres. On the other hand, if they want their thrills to be more intellectual in nature and contain more puzzles, they'll seek out a mystery.

If they want to be transported to a world that's filled with magic, they'll be on the prowl for a fantasy. If they want to be transported to a world that's filled with technological advances (and to grapple with the moral dilemmas these advances create), they'll be on the prowl for science-fiction.

So far, I've kept this presentation simple, describing only one genre at a time. But audience needs can be more complex. Genres can be combined into hybrids. Popular ones include: action comedy, romantic comedy, romantic thriller, and action fantasy.

Also, genre is further divided into smaller categories, or subgenres. A fan of psychological thrillers might have zero interest not only in romances but also in techno-thrillers.

Someone may devour Regency romances, but ignore romances that take place in other historical periods as well as contemporary romances—not to mention thrillers, horror, and science-fiction.

What does this mean for you?

For starters, it means that the size of your target audience is limited. No matter how well-executed your story is, there's always going to be a group of people who simply have no interest in reading (or watching) it—for the time being, at least.

Audience needs are constantly in flux. One day, a reader might be in the mood for a lighthearted romance, but the next day, your lighthearted romance will hold no appeal for her because she's craving a heart-pounding thriller.

Basically, you shouldn't view genre selection as a restriction, designed to box in your creativity. Rather, consider it a signal, a homing beacon that attracts the buyers interested in what you have to sell.

Once you attract this group, you have to make good on your promise. Going into further detail is beyond the scope of this book. For now, just recognize that your story must provide—in sufficient quantities—the genre element(s) audiences are looking for. Otherwise, the pitchforks come out.

Of course, to provide these elements, you first have to pick a genre. This isn't always entirely straightforward because the same concept and plot can lend itself to two vastly different genres.

Look at the fairy tale of Snow White. In 2012, two retellings were released, *Snow White & the Huntsman* and *Mirror Mirror*. Both stories share the same plot: Snow White must overthrow the queen who has stolen Snow's kingdom from her. Their casts share key characters: Snow, the queen, the queen's second-in-command, a prince, and an assortment of dwarves.

But critically, they don't share the same genre. *Huntsman* is an action-adventure fantasy; *Mirror* a fantasy comedy. Thus, despite their core similarities, each film yields an emotional experience that is poles apart from the other.

In *Huntsman*, swordplay results in bloodshed. In *Mirror*, the only casualty is Snow White's outfit. In *Huntsman*, the prince is a master bowman, ready to take up arms to help Snow White reclaim her throne. In *Mirror*, the prince is swindled out of his clothing—twice—by the dwarves and, bizarrely, due to an enchantment, behaves like a dog.

In *Huntsman*, the queen's adjutant is creepy and menacing (and ultimately impaled); in *Mirror*…well, need I go on?

You get the picture. The genre you pick will determine several of your storytelling decisions.

Choose wisely!

ACTION STEP(S)

(7) Cast your plot into a genre mold.

Pick one genre (or a combination with a proven track record). If you're having difficulties, use the following list as a starting point.

Note: This list is not meant to be exhaustive; nor does it include subgenres.

- romance
- drama

- comedy
- action or action-adventure
- thriller
- mystery
- science-fiction
- fantasy
- horror

- chapter six -

LURING AUDIENCES DEEPER STILL VIA THE HOOK

AH, THE HOOK.

The ephemeral ingredient (or a combination of them) that convinces others—book lovers, moviegoers, producers, publishers, actors—to invest time and/or money in your project.

From chapter 5, you know audiences seek out stories in specific genres. It'd be nice if, when they're looking for a romance or a thriller, yours would be one of the few they'd find.

But that's most definitely not the case.

Competition is stiff.

Each genre is filled—nay, overflowing—with other options for audiences to explore and media conglomerates to buy.

The hook is how you convince them to give *your* book, *your* screenplay a chance out of the myriad of possibilities vying for their attention.

In fact, it might be helpful to view the hook through the lens of natural selection. Stories (in a specific genre) are born every day, all the time. Similar to evolutionary adaptations (such as opposable thumbs, large craniums, etc.), hooks endow some of these stories with advantages that enable them to survive "in the wild."

Particularly captivating hooks will not only survive, but thrive—spawning sequels, franchises, and knockoffs—until their dominion comes to an end, and they are replaced by the latest story "species" that meets the current needs of an ever-changing marketplace.

In short, the hook is doubly beneficial. It helps bookworms and financiers, who are faced with a wealth of options, to make a decision about how to allocate their limited resources.

Hopefully, these decision makers choose to spend their time and money on you. That's the second benefit of having a hook. It puts you in a better position to survive (ideally thrive) in the marketplace.

Now that you're convinced of its value, you're probably wondering, *What exactly constitutes a hook?*

Good question.

A hook can be a lot of things. It comes in all shapes and sizes, such as:

- setting
- character

- origin of material
- tone
- title
- book cover
- reputation of the content creator
- star power
- word of mouth
- irony

More details, below.

SETTING: Technological advances, a sci-fi staple, often transform recognizable landscapes into "hookalicious" settings, such as a world where criminals are arrested *before* they commit a crime (*Minority Report*), or one where teenagers are divided into separate factions (*Divergent*).

For a historical-fiction buff, a particular time period and location (ancient Rome, medieval Scotland, colonial America, pre–Partition India, for instance) can be a hook.

Seasons can be effective too. Readers wanting to get into the holiday spirit may gladly add a novel set during the Christmas season to their shopping carts. However, if this novel didn't take place during Christmastime, readers might not spare it a second glance.

CHARACTER: Compelling, charismatic characters have enduring appeal, hooking new readers, year after year, book after book (or movie after movie). Think James Bond. Sherlock Holmes. Jack Reacher. Miss Marple. John McClane. Anne Shirley. Batman. Robin Hood.

More broadly, certain professional fields can create hookalicious characters. Navy SEALs are like catnip for many a romance reader. Yet others swoon over cowboys and billionaires.

ORIGIN OF MATERIAL: Source material can be a hook. "Based on a true story" can potentially add to the value of your screenplay or novel. (The label also comes with a host of legal issues, so tread with caution.)

Like compelling characters, retellings and remakes of legends (BBC's *Merlin*), myths (the Percy Jackson series), and Jane Austen plots (the *Pride and Prejudice* adaptation starring Keira Knightley, to name one) hold perennial appeal.

Fresh takes on old fairy tales have, relatively recently, become popular, but the trend could lose its ability to hook audiences at any moment. Who can say when?

TONE: Tonal choices can make your story more (or less) attractive to prospective buyers.

The bedroom doors may remain closed in your romance. That's a hook for some, but not for others.

Your novel or screenplay may go into all the gory and gruesome details of a zombie attack. Again, that may be a hook for some, but not for others.

TITLE: A clever or catchy title can instantly hook a prospective buyer, and quite economically, too.

Tessa Dare's *Say Yes to the Marquess* is a great example. Fans of Regency romances don't need to know further details about the plot. The cuteness of the title alone would draw them in.

Back to the Future is one of my favorite titles. The future hasn't occurred yet, so how does one return back to it? Due to this irony (concisely conveyed in four words, no less), the title instantly intrigues.

As a matter of fact, irony is a hook in its own right—an extremely powerful one at that. We'll explore it in more depth in just a second. For now, let's move on to the next hook on our list.

BOOK COVERS: Candy for the eye, a great book cover entices readers to take a chance on a novel they know next to nothing about.

They have no clue about its plot, but the cover is so pretty or so cool, it compels them to open up the book and read a sample.

Notice I said readers know *next to* nothing about the book, besides that it has a pretty (or cool) cover. My word choice is deliberate. Without looking at the book description, readers won't know what the book is about.

However, they aren't completely in the dark. Since great book covers convey genre, readers know what kind of emotional experience they're in for.

CONTENT CREATOR: The reputation of some content creators functions like a great book cover. These creators have developed a track record of quality. They're known for reliably producing material that meets audience expectations. Hence, audiences are willing to buy the work of such content creators without knowing much about the content itself.

In publishing, these are the marquee authors who have brand-name recognition rivaling that of a megacorporation. You know the ones. On the covers of their books, their names are larger than the title. Stephen King, Nora Roberts, John Grisham—these author names are all hooks.

Filmmaking is much more collaborative than publishing. Thus, the role of content creator extends beyond the screenwriter to the director and the producer, to name two. (Actors as well, but I classify them in a separate hook category.)

In addition, in comparison to marquee authors, far fewer filmmakers have become household names. Film buffs may know who they are (and flock to their product), but the general public, more often than not, doesn't.

To focus specifically on directors, James Cameron, Steven Spielberg, Martin Scorsese, and Clint Eastwood—their names have made the cut and can be considered hooks to a meaningful proportion of the public.

While some studios have enviable brand-name recognition, others do not. It doesn't really matter. Hardly any have the ability to hook the general public—Pixar and Disney being two noteworthy exceptions.

All the same, as a screenwriter hoping to sell your spec or a novelist hoping Hollywood will adapt your book, *you* have to give some consideration toward hooking the studios (without becoming obsessive about it).

In the simplest scenario, the quality of your material alone will do the trick. More than likely, the path to production will be less direct and more convoluted.

Some aspect of your screenplay, for instance, may hook a director, and then the attachment of the director will hook a top actor, and that combination, hopefully, will hook a studio, convincing it to invest time and money into the project.

Which brings us to…

STAR POWER: Like content creators, actors shape a project, putting their own stamp and voice on it. But since they're significantly more visible, I group actors under their own hook category of *star power*.

Possessing talent and charisma (and usually extremely attractive to boot), actors can draw audiences to their films based on their name alone. Even so, star power is constantly in flux. Burning brightly today, it can burn out tomorrow.

Even actors whose star power is still hot right now are probably unable to attract the sizable audiences they could 15–20 years ago. At least in the United States.

The star power of some actors is potent enough to draw sizeable crowds abroad, enabling studios to handsomely recoup their investment. Because of this factor, star power can't be dismissed as a hook.

That said, in recent times, Hollywood has adopted an alternative approach: hire a young actor who barely registers on the star-power meter, and cast him as a character who's a thousand times more recognizable than the actor is. In essence, the popularity of the character would be the hook to draw in audiences, rather than the star power of the actor.

As Alex French describes it in the *New York Times*:

> **In the new action-hero economy, though, actors rarely carry**

> the franchise; more often, the franchise carries the actor. Chris Hemsworth was little known before *Thor*, and no one outside the industry was too familiar with Henry Cavill before *Man of Steel*. [2]

One last point, just for novelists: for hardcore audiobook listeners, certain narrators (similar to actors) possess star power. These listeners might give the audio version of your book a try, based on the name of the narrator alone. If you're in a position to negotiate who's going to narrate your novel, keep this in mind.

WORD OF MOUTH: Not everyone would classify a word-of-mouth recommendation as a hook. But it is, and a mighty one at that.

Most audience members aren't keen to part with their money or time. But the recommendation from the right person—a trusted friend, a respected colleague—can wear down their resistance in an instant. As BookBub, a book discovery site, observes:

> Readers love getting book recommendations from people they trust…close to 50% of BookBub's members say it's one of the primary ways they find new books to buy. [3]

Or, as David Gaughran put it in *Strangers to Superfans: A Marketing Guide to the Reader Journey*:

> You can engineer any number of sales with smart marketing, but it's even better to have a reader army doing the evangelizing for you, as nothing is more compelling than a fellow reader recommending a book.

Vexingly, this state of affairs results in a "chicken or egg" cycle. Before people can recommend your story and hook others, they first have to give your screenplay or novel a chance.

They have to be hooked themselves.

With no one recommending your story to them, how do you accomplish this? You have to lure them in with other hooks—especially the one we have yet to discuss: irony.

5 Surefire Ways to Make Your Story Idea More Ironic

Irony is irresistible.

It's one of the most powerful hooks in your arsenal. A magnetic force, it draws audiences to it. They become keener to part with their time and money in order to experience it.

If you're not an irony grand master, don't worry. I'm about to share specific techniques you can use to sharpen your ironic eye and create an audience magnet of your own.

And if you are an irony grand master, you probably use these techniques instinctively, without giving it a second thought. If that's the case, you might want to skip ahead to the next section, "Intrinsic vs. Extrinsic Hooks."

To master irony, it first helps to understand what it is. To incorporate irony at the conceptual level (as opposed to the dialogue or scene level), I've found this working definition to be helpful: it's the juxtaposition of opposites.

In other words, your story concept must plausibly pair at least two opposing elements that audiences wouldn't, as a general rule, expect to encounter together.

This isn't just a practical definition of irony, it's the source of irony's allure. The unexpectedness of the combination arouses audience curiosity, as they contemplate how these two opposites will be reconciled.

The more you can tap into this wellspring of curiosity, the greater competitive advantage your story is going to have.

But how to go about it? How to find a pairing whose unexpectedness will entice audiences to give your screenplay or novel a chance?

Until your instinct for irony becomes well honed, try one of the five combinations discussed in the following pages. All are regularly used to good effect.

Two quick caveats: this set of ironic combinations is intended to get you on the right track. It's not meant to be exhaustive. Also, some combinations may not apply to your genre.

Okay, let's dive in!

Irony Combination #1: Most Competency + Least Likely

There are two basic variations of this irony combination.

In the first variation, the protagonist faces a problem; but, *due to* his considerable, relevant expertise, he's the least likely person to be in such a predicament. In the second variation, the protagonist must solve a problem. Yet, *despite* his considerable, relevant expertise, he'd be the candidate least likely to be chosen.

In the world of *Minority Report*, criminals are arrested based on intention, before they actually commit a crime. When the protagonist is about to be arrested for a murder he didn't intend to commit, he must go on the run and prove his innocence.

This protagonist, Anderton, isn't a regular citizen. He's in charge of the Precrime police. He's supposed to *prevent* murder and chase down possible criminals, not commit murder (technically, not intend to commit murder) and go on the lam himself.

Hence, he's the least likely—and most ironic—person to be targeted by his Precrime colleagues. Fortunately, his insider knowledge (i.e. competency) provides him with the skills necessary to cope with his situation.

Theoretically, someone close to Anderton (like his estranged wife) could be targeted instead. While this situation is ironic too (the man responsible for stopping crime is apparently married to a criminal), it's not ironic to the same degree. It's ironic via proxy.

Watch out for this. In most cases, irony via proxy isn't going to be as compelling as taking it all the way. When you're brainstorming possibilities, you may be so pleased that you made your concept more ironic (via proxy), you may not realize that it's probably necessary to go one step further.

Minority Report is an example of the first variation of combining "the protagonist least likely" with competency. As an example of the second, let's revisit *Speed*. Remember our discussion from chapters 2 and 3?

Assuming the concept is developed as an action movie (not a

comedy), the protagonist must be someone who's physically fit and has experience with explosives.

In the film, Jack is part of the LAPD SWAT team. He didn't have to be, mind you. Another government agency could fit the bill just as well. Jack could've been an ex-marine or an FBI agent or part of an ATF task force.

That's one route to take, and it's certainly proven successful. However, if we want to make the premise more ironic, then we'd have to look for less typical alternatives. Instead of going for the "most likely" protagonist, we'd switch gears and brainstorm "least likely" possibilities.

Who could be physically fit and have experience with explosives, but would be least likely to be chosen to stop a terrorist plot?

Another terrorist, of course.

How ironic. A terrorist is used to stop another terrorist from detonating a bomb. It's the reverse of the *Minority Report* setup. The person you'd expect to commit a crime is now trying to stop one.

For a more lighthearted (but equally ironic) take, examine *White Collar*. A con man is used by the FBI to apprehend other con men. As one tagline for the TV show goes, "To catch a thief, it helps to be one."

One quick pointer before we move on. This irony combination (most competency + least likely) is great to lend credibility to your premise, while still leaving the door open for character development. Phrased differently: to explore your protagonist's growth, you won't use his improvement in a particular skill set. Rather, you'll use his *reluctance* to embrace his (already well developed) skills.

Irony Combination #2: Varying Degrees of Competency + New Waters

As you've probably guessed, this kind of ironic pairing is the bedrock of "fish out of water" concepts, in which the protagonist is thrown into a new environment (which I think of as *new waters*).

I want to stress that this new environment doesn't have to be physically different from the protagonist's old one (although it often is). The protagonist can also be tossed into "metaphysical" new waters, where he experiences a change in state or being.

Liar Liar is a good example of this. Fletcher's inability to tell lies for 24 hours doesn't necessitate traveling to a new location. Nevertheless, as a profligate liar, Fletcher's in uncharted territory. He's in a world that's completely foreign to him, the equivalent of being tossed into a foreign country like India, for example.

In addition to new waters, to generate irony, something from the protagonist's everyday world just doesn't mesh with his new one.

There are different ways to go about this. As with irony combination #1 (most competency + least likely), I find it helpful to think in terms of competency.

In one variation, the protagonist is thrown into new waters to solve a problem, and this problem requires a skill set that he uses regularly in his everyday world. Hence, the irony isn't produced by the difference between his field of competency and the problem at hand. Instead, it's produced by his attitude, which is, in some way, at odds with his new environment.

In *Beverly Hills Cop*, Alex Foley is a decent Detroit detective (the botched chase at the movie's beginning, notwithstanding). His investigative skills are relevant to his goal: to go to Beverly Hills (new waters) to figure out who murdered his childhood friend.

So far, there's nothing unexpected or unusual about the combination of these elements. The irony is caused through Foley's attitude. He's exuberant and unorthodox, and his investigative style clashes with the stuffy Beverly Hills police officers who always play by the book.

Likewise, in *The Heat*, although Sarah and Shannon have shortcomings (Sarah is arrogant; Shannon is aggressive; neither is well liked by their colleagues), as agents of the law, they get results. No surprise that they're applying their skills to bust a drug ring.

If they were working individually to accomplish this goal, the premise wouldn't contain any irony. But since they're working together—and since their problem-solving styles vastly differ—they're at odds with each other, and this is what makes the concept both ironic and humorous.

In this example, in contrast to *Beverly Hills Cop*, note that the new waters are metaphysical: a partnership between two people who're much better at operating alone. It doesn't matter that Sarah relocates to Boston to work on the case. It's being *with Shannon*, not *in Boston* that generates the irony.

Both *Beverly Hills Cop* and *The Heat* are action comedies. But irony combination #2 can be applied to other genres as well. Take *Jaws*. Police Chief Martin Brody is literally tossed into new waters, where he must kill the great white shark terrorizing the citizens of Amity.

Unlike Quint and Hooper, Brody doesn't have shark-specific experience. Despite this, I'd classify him as competent to handle the task at hand because (1) he's a seasoned officer of the law and (2) this experience relates to his duty to protect Amity. It's not Brody's competency, but his attitude—his fear of the water—that puts him at odds with his current situation.

In other kinds of stories, the irony is generated by the difference between the protagonist's field of competency and his predicament. That is to say, in his everyday world, he possesses a skill set that seemingly has no bearing on the problem he must solve in his new environment.

More often than not, this skill set is diametrically opposed to his new world, rendering him the person least likely to succeed. However, by the end of the story, he'll find a way to reconcile the two, arriving at a successful outcome that probably wouldn't have occurred if he had possessed the relevant skills to begin with.

For example:

- In *The Pacifier*, Shane's navy SEAL tactical training seems incompatible with his new assignment: to babysit five children.
- In *Miss Congeniality*, Gracie's FBI training (and her tomboyish nature) don't jive with the ultrafeminine beauty pageant she must infiltrate.
- In *The Internship*, the old school, "analog" techniques of two salesmen seem out of place in the high-tech headquarters of the internet behemoth they now work for.

Yet, by the end of all three of these films, the protagonists are able to unite two disparate skill sets and achieve victory.

Finally, there are stories where it's uncharitable, even inaccurate to say that the protagonist is incompetent. At the same time, in his everyday world, he doesn't appear to have specialized skills. He's just a regular guy, an average Joe, who's been tossed into a situation far out of his comfort zone. Alternatively, if he does have specialized skills they either (a) aren't depicted at all or (b) have no bearing on the plot.

Think of *Date Night*, where a suburban couple gets caught up in a ring of corruption. *Bait and Switch*, a.k.a. *The Swap*, a project Mark Wahlberg's interested in, seems to follow a similar pattern. As described by the Tracking Board, it's about "a couple who swap houses with another couple in Bali, only to discover that they're staying in the home of the world's most sought-after spies, forcing them to take up arms against the onslaught of highly trained assassins." [4]

Note: I haven't read the script, but because *Bait and Switch* is billed as an action *comedy*, I assume the house-swapping couple, unlike their adversaries, are not trained assassins—and like *Date Night*'s Phil and Claire, are completely ill-equipped to handle their problem.

Irony Combination #3: Untested Competency + Least Likely

Here, the protagonist is a novice. He's green, wet behind the ears.

Sure, he's read the manual, taken the tests, and participated in the drills. But he lacks practical knowledge and experience. He hasn't been out in the field.

Now, though, he's thrown into it. He's assigned a case or mission that even someone with a decade's worth of experience would have difficulty tackling. Therein lies the irony.

Look at *Safe House*. Tobin Frost is a CIA agent who's gone rogue, selling secrets to the highest bidder. When Frost waltzes into the American consul in South Africa, the CIA wants to know why.

An agent with extensive experience would have trouble handling Frost, who's an "expert manipulator of human assets." But Frost isn't guarded by someone with experience; he's guarded by Matt Weston, a green agent who's frustrated because of how little action he's seen.

When reading this description, you probably didn't jump out of your seat and say, "Oh, that's a movie I'd like to see." And I'd agree. To be effective, this irony combination usually needs some extra juice from another hook (ironic or otherwise).

Take *My Cousin Vinny*. Although Vinny presumably studied criminal law in law school, he has no actual experience with it. To be more accurate, Vinny has little experience, period. He's only been practicing law for a mere 6 weeks, and in this short time span, he's never gone to trial.

Being such a novice with regard to the law in general and completely lacking experience with criminal law in particular, Vinny's the least likely candidate to defend his cousin (and his cousin's buddy), who have been accused of murdering a store clerk.

If you're familiar with the film, you know that Vinny's inexperience isn't the film's only source of irony. He's a fish out of water, too: a brash, tough-talking New Yorker who's been transplanted to Alabama, where he (and his girlfriend) stick out like sore thumbs.

Imagine what the film would be like if one of these sources of irony were removed. Vinny would still be a neophyte who bumbles his way through the arraignment and bungles his opening statement…but the case takes place in New York, or another metropolitan city like Chicago or Las Vegas.

Alternatively, Vinny's a fish out of water, transplanted to Alabama from New York, still completely dumbfounded by grits…but he does have extensive trial experience.

It's not quite the same, is it?

Either way, the story loses some of its appeal. Both sources of irony must be present to maximize the concept's potential.

This illustrates a good point: once you develop a knack for integrating irony into your concept, you should cultivate the skill of layering *multiple* sources of irony into it, thereby maximizing its magnetism. Bear in mind, there is an upper limit to how many hooks a concept can contain. (As a matter of fact, we'll discuss this topic later on in this chapter.)

I also include Walter Mitty and ivory-tower types in this irony combination (untested competency + least likely). Like their green, wet-behind-the-ear counterparts, these characters don't have field experience. However, in contrast to green novices, their training comes purely from fantasy, not reality—rendering them woefully (and often comically) underprepared for their journey.

Consider Joan in *Romancing the Stone*. As a romance novelist, she regularly fantasizes about tough, sassy heroines who go on wild adventures, but she's never been on an adventure herself. In fact, she is shy and retiring, safely cloistered away in her New York apartment. That all changes when her sister is kidnapped, and Joan is forced to go on an adventure that could've come straight from the pages of one of her bestsellers.

Like Joan, *Kung Fu Panda*'s Po also has an active imagination. In his dreams, he's a kung fu master. But in reality, he's an overweight, soup-selling panda—falling far short of the mark established by his kung fu idols. Hence, it's ironic that he, out of the entire populace, is chosen as the Dragon Warrior who'll save his village from the villain.

Irony Combination #4: Competency with Others + Incompetency with Self

Physician, heal thyself.

This expression is the perfect—and pithy—way to describe this irony combination, where everyone but the protagonist can benefit from the protagonist's expertise.

Technically, this circumstance can be classified under irony combination #1 (most competency + least likely), but it's specialized enough to warrant its own category.

When dating guru *Hitch* orchestrates dates for his clients, everything goes according to plan. But when Hitch is struck by Cupid's arrow, and tries to woo a woman for his own, everything goes haywire. (*Note*: *Hitch* also incorporates irony combo #5, but we haven't gotten there yet!)

Here's another example, from a project that was in development. (I'm not sure about its status now.) In this case, the protagonist is literally a physician—a Hollywood pediatrician—who "thought he had the baby thing covered, until it happened to him." [5]

Poor guy; great concept!

This next example illustrates how you can use irony to develop a procedural for television. Produced by Shonda Rhimes, *The Catch* is a show about a female fraud investigator who's about to be victimized by her fiancé. She must find the liar before he destroys her career.

Ironic, isn't it?

Presumably, if the heroine were hired by a female client to investigate the client's fiancé, the heroine would immediately detect if the fiancé were brimming with deceit.

Unfortunately, similar to the Hollywood pediatrician, the heroine couldn't use her skills to protect herself—landing her in a precarious position, which I presume, is the source for the serial element of the procedural.

One last example, this time from Nina George's novel, *The Little Paris Bookshop*. The protagonist owns a floating bookshop (a barge on the Seine). In addition, he acts like a therapist to the brokenhearted, prescribing the perfect book to help them overcome their pain.

These two elements are great hooks. To top it off, the author added a third—this one, ironic. The protagonist, sadly, cannot benefit from his own talent. As described in the cover copy, "The only person he can't seem to heal through literature is himself; he's still haunted by heartbreak after his great love disappeared."

Irony Combination #5: Attraction + Least Likely

Many a romance is built on this combination of irony, where two people who are the least likely to be in a relationship find themselves falling in love.

Going back to *Hitch*, Hitch's relationship predicament is ironic in more ways than one. That's because Hitch has fallen for a reporter who "lives for the scoop," and she's hot on the trail of a story that could expose his identity as a date doctor. In sum, she's the worst—and thus, most ironic—candidate for his affection.

You can get to this endpoint in a couple of ways. One is to start with a romantic duo in mind, and work backward.

Say you're writing a new-adult romance novel. In it, a rock star moves next door to the heroine. Rock stars are a hot commodity in this genre, and the premise taps into the kind of wish-fulfillment fantasy that appeals to your target audience. Coupled with a sizzling cover, that may be enough to get a reader to buy your book, or, at the very least, read a few sample chapters.

But if you take things even further, and make your premise more ironic, your book may become downright irresistible.

How to do that?

Simple. Just think about what kind of person would *least* want to be in a relationship with a rock star.

In theory, it'd be fun, glamorous even, to date a sexy, wealthy musician. But the perks come with drawbacks; loss of privacy being a biggie. And there's our source of irony: a rock star, who's always in the spotlight, falls for a girl who'd do anything to avoid it.

Oh yeah. That's instantly more compelling, isn't it? Even if rock-star romances aren't your thing, you can probably see how this concept would be a magnet for those who do like them.

Notice that when you reflect on why the heroine is so publicity shy, other pieces of your story will start to fall into place.

Maybe there's a tragedy that happened in the past, and she doesn't want the media to dredge it up, and make her family headline news again.

Maybe her dad is running for governor, and a romance with the rock star would attract the kind of attention that could jeopardize her dad's political campaign.

Either one makes for great stakes. Not only that, they're also strong subplot material. The slow reveal of the past tragedy, the ups and downs of the dad's political campaign—both could provide relief from the romance plot, preventing the story from becoming monotonous.

There's another method to arrive at the attraction + least likely irony combination. It's best suited for romances where neither the hero nor the heroine is actively seeking love. Indeed, we covered most of the process in action step #5. Now it's time to add the crowning—ironic—touch.

To quickly review the process: start with one protagonist; the heroine, for instance. Give her a SMART goal. Then, create an antagonist who could thwart this SMART goal.

Finally (and this is the new step), *make this antagonist the hero.* (You might have to change the gender of the SMART-goal antagonist to accomplish this.)

Thus, the heroine falls for her sworn enemy, the least likely candidate for her affection—and the most ironic.

Voila! Instant hook.

To illustrate, let's run through the process right now. We'll start with a heroine. A single mother, perhaps. Her goal? Anything that strikes our fancy.

Maybe, as you're brainstorming, you remember that the previous winter created huge pot holes on several city streets...and how your normally calm neighbors became incensed over the issue. This memory becomes the inspiration behind your heroine's SMART goal: to run for mayor.

Conveniently, this goal comes with a whole host of possible antagonists. The heroine's main political rival is the most obvious. But key players, like his campaign manager or his top donor, work too. To keep things simple, we'll choose her political rival.

To make our story ironic, we just have to follow the last step and—drumroll, please!—make her political rival her love interest. Here's our final version: a single mother runs for mayor of a small city, but her campaign is jeopardized when she falls in love with her biggest political rival.

If ironic situations come naturally to you, this result may've seemed painfully obvious from the second I said our heroine was running for office. But if you have difficulty coming up with ironic plots for your romances, this methodical, regimented approach will serve you well.

One more point: while you can use this method for romances where the hero and/or heroine are actively pursuing a romance with each other, it takes quite a bit of finessing. That's because it's not very believable for either protagonist to pursue a relationship with someone who poses a threat to him or her. To make the romance credible, an element of anonymity is usually required.

In *You've Got Mail*, Kathleen exchanges emails with a stranger, never realizing that he's the owner of a bookstore chain that's endangering the future of her children's bookshop. However, because they agreed not to share personal details with each other (he only knows her as Shopgirl; she only knows him as NY152), she doesn't look foolish for seeking companionship from the man who can threaten her livelihood and legacy (the shop was passed down to her from her mother).

So far, our examples have been concentrated within lighthearted fare. But irony combination #5 can be applied to grittier tales. In *Out of Sight* and *The Town*, the protagonists (both of whom are thieves) fall in love with women (a federal marshal and a witness to a bank robbery, respectively) who can send them to jail.

• • •

With the above set of irony combinations, you should be able to quickly identify ways to amplify the irony of your story idea. Remember, though, that this list isn't exhaustive. If these specific combinations don't work for you, it may be more useful to think more generally.

Go back to our original definition of irony and focus on its core: providing a combination that goes against expectation.

For instance, governments are supposed to protect the people. If you assign a behavior to them that's contrary to expectation, like let's say, killing citizens, then you'll be tapping into the same irony that's partly at the heart of *The Hunger Games* and *Absolute Power*.

Intrinsic vs. Extrinsic Hooks

In my mind, hooks fall into two camps: intrinsic and extrinsic.

Intrinsic hooks are part of the content of a screenplay or novel itself. They're almost always under your control.

Extrinsic hooks, on the other hand, are connected to the content, emerging from it, but aren't part of the content itself. Barring specific circumstances (e.g. you're self-publishing your novel), they're usually not under your control.

These are intrinsic hooks:

- setting
- character
- origin of material
- tone
- title
- irony

These are extrinsic hooks:

- book cover
- reputation of the content creator
- star power
- word of mouth

For whatever reason, some writers tend to focus—excessively—on extrinsic hooks.

They stress over the number of reviews their book has, worrying about its current lack of social proof. Or, after reading a tidbit in the trades, they wonder how they're ever going to hook both a director and a top actor in order to hook a studio, which, apparently, is making fewer films this year than ever before.

This mindset isn't just unproductive, it's also shortsighted. Remember, extrinsic hooks emerge from intrinsic ones. When intrinsic hooks are absent or of low quality, extrinsic hooks are likely to be lacking, too. Conversely, a plethora of high-quality intrinsic hooks should result in extrinsic hooks, making your work even more appealing to book buyers or studios.

That's not all. In some cases, the magnetic appeal of an extrinsic hook may be limited by an intrinsic hook. Here's an example of what I mean. Agatha Christie is a marquee author. For me, her allure, although great, is still limited. I'll devour anything she's written—as long as it stars either Hercule Poirot or Miss Marple (character hooks).

Same for mystery writer Elizabeth George. I'll buy an Inspector

Lynley mystery (at least the ones starring Lynley or Havers) without a second thought, but her other fiction offerings have never made it (at least not yet) into my shopping cart. Here again, the intrinsic hook of compelling characters supersedes the extrinsic hook of the author's reputation.

Finally, and most important, because extrinsic hooks aren't under a writer's direct control, obsessing about them can make one feel powerless. That's not only frustrating, it can also be damaging—causing depression, or otherwise adversely affecting mental well-being, through a psychological phenomenon known as learned helplessness.

For the sake of your own sanity, if you find yourself stewing over extrinsic hooks—or indeed, any part of the production process that's out of your control—shift your focus back onto intrinsic hooks and the things that you *can* control. If not for your current project (because it's too late to change its content), then for the next one.

Remember that irony is one of the most potent hooks there is—and *it's completely under your control.*

You determine how ironic your concept is.

Not anyone else.

When you're feeling discouraged, let this knowledge empower you.

If you take this advice to heart, then at this moment, you're probably asking yourself a critical question—

How Hookalicious Does a Story Have to Be?

We've mostly danced around this before, but let's mention it explicitly now: stories can have, and usually do have, more than one hook.

As aforementioned, BBC's *Merlin* hooks audiences through the King Arthur angle. But it contains at least four other hooks, too:

(1) In this fantasy realm, magic is outlawed (setting).

(2) Magicians like Merlin are not supposed to perform magic (irony). (Observe that this hook is a byproduct of the setting hook.)

(3) If a prospective viewer's fondness for all things *Buffy* extends to actor Anthony Head, then his presence in the cast would be a hook (star power).

(4) It's a clean, gore-free, and cross-generational show that can be watched by children and their parents and grandparents (tone).

Glancing at this list, you may conclude that the more hooks your story has, the more the odds are stacked in your favor. Many times that's true, but it isn't always the case.

To see why, let's conduct another hook analysis, this time for *The Proposal*. By my count, the romantic comedy has at least four hooks going for it:

(1) Margaret's the boss, while Andrew is her overworked assistant. (The gender reversal goes against expectation.)

(2) Margaret, a high-strung New Yorker, is thrown into the low-key environs of Sitka, Alaska (i.e. she's a fish out of water).

(3) Margaret and Andrew have to pretend they adore each other, even though their working relationship isn't all sunshine and rainbows (irony via fake engagement).

(4) Margaret is played by Sandra Bullock; Andrew by Ryan Reynolds (star power).

That last one is an extrinsic hook. For our purposes, we can ignore it, leaving us with three.

Take note of two things. One, all of these hooks "play nice" with each other. Relocating the fake engagement to Sitka, for instance, doesn't require undue contrivance. Put another way, the screenwriter didn't have to "stretch" the plot in order to accommodate it.

Two, medium plays a role in determining hook quantity. As a film, *The Proposal* had to contain multiple hooks in order to attract the millions of dollars required to produce it. A novel, however, could skate by on less. The fake engagement alone could bring a romance novelist reasonable success.

But before you settle on a single-hook story, put yourself in the shoes of a romance reader. Given the choice, which would be more likely to entice her to dip into her pocketbook?

Option A: A romance novel with just the fake-engagement hook.

Option B: A romance novel with the fake engagement, gender reversal, *and* fish-out-of-water combo.

Did you say Option B?

Yeah, me too.

To sum it up, in some situations, multiple hooks may be less of a necessity, but still, nevertheless, advantageous. Conversely, in other situations, compressing multiple hooks into a story can do more harm than good.

Think about our ironic take on *Speed*: a terrorist must stop another terrorist, who's rigged a bomb to explode on a bus when the bus goes below 50 mph.

Does our additional hook improve this concept or not?

To evaluate its merits, let's address the 50-mph aspect first. *Speed* has dibs on that. We can't use it, not if we want to avoid the copycat label. But for the sake of argument, let's assume that it's ours for the taking.

A bomb on a bus.

Look at the shape of this story. Due to the speed requirement, for the most part, all the action is going to be contained within, or immediately exterior to, the bus. The excitement comes from watching the protagonist keep the bus above 50 mph.

He doesn't need to have past experience as a terrorist to do that.

We can't really make use of our modification, as ironic as it is. If we try to work our protagonist's backstory into the plot, it would probably feel extraneous. On the other hand, if we don't allude to our protagonist's past as a terrorist, then audiences would wonder why we cast a terrorist as the protagonist in the first place.

In short, while we have more irony, we do not have a better story. We've got ourselves hook overload.

The terrorist-vs.-terrorist hook just isn't conducive to being explored simultaneously with the bomb-on-a-speeding-bus hook. The former is better suited to a premise in which the majority of the action *isn't* tied to a single, small location, thereby providing more opportunities for our protagonist's past history to bear relevance.

In this case, a single hook—a crowded bus must maintain a speed of at least 50 mph or it will explode—suffices. In contrast to our *Proposal* example, medium doesn't make a difference. Whether the end product is a novel or a screenplay, adding more hooks is not only unnecessary, it's liable to detract from the power of the original hook.

ACTION STEP(S)

(8) Settle on a setting (place, time period, and season).

Choose a setting for your story. Ideally, it should be hookalicious, but this isn't always possible, or necessary.

Regardless, you still need to choose somewhere specific, if only to prevent boring audiences with generic backdrops for your scenes.

If you're writing science-fiction or fantasy, spend a little time worldbuilding now. But save more intensive efforts for when you've completed your outline.

Then you'll be in better shape to determine whether, for instance, it's really essential to know how your protagonist's homeland evolved into a republic. This is only a suggestion, however. Disregard it if it doesn't work for you.

(9) Assess your story's intrinsic appeal.

List all the intrinsic hooks contained within your story. As a refresher, intrinsic hooks include: setting, character, origin of material, tone, title, and irony.

This list should help you (a) understand how commercially viable your story is and (b) complete action steps #10 and #11.

(10) Amplify the irony.

Modify your protagonist, his predicament, his antagonist, the setting, or a combination of these to increase the irony of your concept.

If you're stuck, try incorporating one of the five irony combos we discussed in this chapter.

Follow this action step, even if your idea is ironic already. You never know, there might be something you overlooked the first time around. Say you've transplanted your protagonist into new waters. That's a great start, but your concept might be even better if you also make your protagonist a novice who lacks practical experience (à la *My Cousin Vinny*).

Additionally, if, to increase the irony of your concept, you've had to make your protagonist more of a "bungler," spend a little time reflecting on your credibility strategy (as discussed in action step #4).

(11) Evaluate the hooks in your story, together, as a group.

Does your story have enough room for all of your hooks? Can they coexist together, under the same roof, without distorting the shape of your "house"?

Answering this question may mean that you have to discard (a) the extra irony you injected into your concept in action step #10 or (b) another element of your story.

Don't be sad, though. Save whatever you discard for another project!

Second, consult the list you created in action step #9 and verify that your concept has enough hooks to be a worthwhile investment.

If you're writing a screenplay, does it have enough appeal to justify a multimillion-dollar budget?

If you're writing a novel with a niche audience (hardcore Sherlock Holmes fans, let's say), does it have enough appeal to attract (a) Holmes fans as well as (b) readers who aren't as keen on Holmes…but who are always looking for a well-written whodunit?

If your answer to questions like these is no, add more hooks (while keeping cohesion in mind), until the answer is yes!

• • •

For all this talk of hooks, remember that a hook is a necessary, but insufficient condition for success. It's a gateway, something that inspires potential buyers to pluck your story from the masses.

It doesn't obligate them to keep reading.

No, to do that, you've got to follow through. You have to fulfill their expectations and prove that your story *is* worth their time and money. Many elements are involved in accomplishing this objective. One of the most critical—story structure—is the topic of Part II of this writing guide.

But before we venture there, we must address the final step in popping the story kernel: the logline.

- chapter seven -

SUMMARIZING YOUR STORY IN ONE SENTENCE VIA THE LOGLINE

IF YOU'RE A SCREENWRITER, YOU'RE PROBABLY already acquainted with Monsieur Logline. If you're a novelist, this may be your first introduction to him.

Basically, the logline is a one-sentence description of your story.

One sentence.

That's it.

Not a lot, granted. But it's enough.

As a matter of fact, if you can't corral the gist of your story into one sentence, it may indicate that you're trying to cram too much into your screenplay or novel, even though it doesn't have room for it.

There are exceptions, of course. Generally speaking, though, if you can't form a coherent, cohesive sentence out of your story's key ingredients, they're unlikely to yield a coherent, cohesive draft.

Speaking of a rough draft, summarizing it in 30–50 words (or thereabouts) can seem like a daunting task—more difficult than actually producing your 100-page screenplay or 100,000-word novel.

Don't sweat it.

Seriously.

By completing the previous action steps, you've already done most of the work. All you have to do is plug your answers into the template I'm about to share.

Ready?

Here it is, in its bare-bones form: because of a compelling reason, a protagonist must accomplish a goal—despite extraordinary resistance.

Now, a slightly modified version, with the appropriate action steps indicated in brackets: because of the stakes [action step #6], a protagonist [action steps #2 and #3b] must accomplish a goal [action step #2]—despite the antagonistic forces in his way [action step #3a].

A few things to keep in mind: to produce a sentence that makes sense, you may have to tweak the grammar a bit or alter the order of the components (e.g. leading with the antagonist, instead of ending the logline with him).

Also, sometimes you can omit certain elements (usually the stakes) because they're implied. For instance, in romances, the stakes might only involve the future happiness of the hero and the heroine. You don't need to say that explicitly. In an action movie, if the hero has to stop an explosion, you don't need to add that lives will be saved. That's pretty much a given.

Because you are limited to one sentence, don't try to describe your protagonist's goal using all of its SMART attributes. Be as specific as you can, while balancing clarity with conciseness.

Finally, in most cases, the hook (at least one of them) should be readily apparent, without requiring extra effort on your part. If the hook comes from irony for instance, combining your story elements into one sentence should automatically showcase your pair of chosen opposites.

And if a hook isn't readily apparent by the time you're done with your logline, then find a way to weave one in there!

Below are a few logline examples to get you started:

A FEW GOOD MEN: To prevent two marines from being convicted of murder, a navy lawyer—accustomed to easy victories—must elicit a confession from a powerful colonel desperate to suppress the truth.

ONE FOR THE MONEY: Facing eviction and desperate for cash, a freshly minted female bounty hunter must apprehend a cop accused of murder…who also happens to be her ex-flame.

THE ITALIAN JOB (2003): When his mentor is killed by a greedy associate, a charismatic thief (with help from the mentor's straight-laced daughter) plans to avenge his mentor by stealing the greedy associate's stash of gold bars—worth millions.

THE PROPOSAL: To avoid deportation, a high-maintenance New York editor fakes an engagement to the assistant who despises her, and must convince his family (who resides in Sitka, Alaska) that their romance is real.

AVATAR: A colonel promises to restore a quadriplegic veteran's mobility if the vet infiltrates an extraterrestrial society by using newly developed avatar technology; however, when the vet falls in love with one of the natives, he backtracks on the deal and helps her defend her people from the colonel.

THE TRUMAN SHOW: Unbeknownst to Truman, his whole life has been broadcast to the world in a reality TV show; eventually cottoning on and wishing for freedom, he must escape from the set—a fake island—and outmaneuver the show's executive producer.

Not as hard as you thought it would be, was it?

But why bother?

Why is this task necessary at all?

When you're generating your outline, or even when you're in the midst of writing your rough draft, you'll come up with ideas that will take you in new, unforeseen, unexpected directions.

Such "rabbit trails" can either improve upon or detract from your initial idea. (In fact, making these kinds of evaluations is a big part of stage 2 of iterative outlining.) All the same, you can't go down rabbit trails indefinitely.

There comes a point when you have to settle on the way you're going to develop your story. Once you do, you have to honor the way you've chosen. If you don't, your story is liable to meander off in multiple directions, leaving confused and unhappy audience members in its wake.

This is where the logline comes in. It's a touchstone that will guide you when you're unsure what to do with a particular scene.

Barring other factors, if the scene connects to your logline (sometimes, these connections are rather indirect, as is often the case with subplots), keep it in. If it doesn't—no matter how awesome it is—it belongs on the cutting room floor, so to speak.

That's not all. If you're a screenwriter, your logline can help you succinctly pitch your screenplay to someone who doesn't have the time (nor the inclination) for a lengthier description.

If you're a novelist, your logline can be a springboard, helping you craft a query letter (if you're seeking a traditional publishing deal) or your own cover copy (if you're self-publishing) with relative ease. (PS: Loglines are really handy to describe each individual book in a box set.)

To be clear, the logline template in this chapter is designed to help you plot your screenplay or novel. For pitching or marketing purposes, you'll probably need to provide more context. The template provided here should make the process more manageable.

Use the template to produce a rough cut, then fine-tune as required. For instance, you might need to add a few well-chosen adjectives to convey your story's genre or subtract a few words to improve sentence flow.

Finally, the logline (with a little extra info from this book) will enable you to crack the structural code of your story—making it more enjoyable to read *and* easier to write.

Happily enough, this is the topic of Part II of this writing guide. But first…complete action step #12!

ACTION STEP(S)

(12) Construct a logline for your story.

Using the template in this chapter, combine the key ingredients of your story into one sentence. (Two at the absolute maximum.)

If necessary, refer back to the examples in this chapter for inspiration.

NOTES FOR PART I

Chapter 2

1. *Wikipedia*, s.v. "Little Miss Sunshine," last modified October 6, 2015, https://en.wikipedia.org/wiki/Little_Miss_Sunshine.

Chapter 6

2. Alex French, "The Last, Disposable Action Hero," *New York Times Magazine*, February 28, 2014, http://www.nytimes.com/2014/03/02/magazine/the-last-disposable-action-hero.html.

3. William Green, "BookBub Recommendations: A Free Way for Authors to Engage with Readers on BookBub.com," *BookBub Partners Blog*, March 21, 2018, https://insights.bookbub.com/recommendations.

4. Clark Allen, "Hot *Black Mass* Scribe Jez Butterworth Set to Re-Write Mark Wahlberg's *Bait And Switch*," *Tracking Board* (blog), April 30, 2015, http://www.tracking-board.com/tb-exclusive-hot-black-mass-scribe-jez-butterworth-set-to-re-write-mark-wahlbergs-bait-and-switch/.

5. Jenna Milly, "Matt Allen and Caleb Wilson Write About Eating, Sleeping and Pooping," *Script Magazine*, September 29, 2010, http://www.scriptmag.com/features/matt-allen-and-caleb-wilson-write-about-eating-sleeping-and-pooping.

- PART II -

HOW TO BUILD YOUR STORY STRUCTURE, A.K.A. CRACKING YOUR STORY CODE

To QUICKLY RECAP, WITH YOUR LOGLINE IN HAND, YOU HAVE:

- a protagonist through whom audiences can experience your story
- at least one antagonist to provide the kind of conflict that keeps audiences entertained
- stakes that will secure audiences' emotional involvement
- genre and at least one hook, which, coupled together, should reel in audiences
- a SMART goal—the umbrella that houses all the elements, anchors your story, and prevents audience attention from drifting away

Basically, you've made inroads toward creating a screenplay or novel worth reading. You've taken your original burst of inspiration and developed it into a decent story idea.

Nevertheless, a decent idea—even a brilliant one—can collapse due to weak structure.

As readers and moviegoers, we've all had that experience: being hooked by an amazing concept, being so excited to dive into it, only to be disappointed by its execution.

While many factors play a role in delighting audiences, structure is one of the most critical. With strong structure in place, you won't take forever to get your story "off the ground"; you won't blow the good stuff too soon; and you'll bring everything together in a satisfying conclusion.

By figuring out the structure of your story in advance (in particular the midpoint and the end of Act Two), your story won't remain static. It won't feel the same on page 35 as it does on page 75 (in a screenplay) or page 325 (in a novel).

It won't just advance forward; it will get progressively more interesting.

Quality stuff, that.

But before you can even worry about whether your story captivates audiences from beginning till end, you've got to write the darn thing.

Although valuable, your logline has shortcomings. It is only one sentence after all. By itself, it's not much of a defense against the blank page.

Even with it, you're likely to stare at your computer screen…

…asking yourself that dreaded question, *What happens next?*

Maybe not at first, but at some point, you'll stop typing because you don't know how to advance your story forward.

Panic sets in.

To alleviate it, you engage in the time-old panacea of procrastination.

You know the drill. You twiddle around on your favorite social media platform, read indignant comments on your favorite blogs, order something online because it's easy to buy, daydream about what you're going to do with the money you'll get when you sell the project you haven't finished yet (don't deny it, we all do it!)—and, if you're feeling really desperate, maybe load up the dishwasher or get started on the laundry.

Instead of writing, you loaf around (or clean your house). And when days pass with no progress in sight, you become discouraged.

Eventually, you just give up.

Another project bites the dust.

Having stuffed it into a storage box, where it joins other false starts, you begin the process of recovery. Finally, you launch a new project—only, once again, you run out of steam one-third, maybe two-thirds, of the way through.

End result: thousands of words that go nowhere.

Take heart.

There is a simple way to avoid this vicious cycle.

Here again, structure is key. With it, you'll know something about the way your story unfolds. Not only that, *your knowledge is interspersed at regular intervals.*

That is to say, you're not just clued in to your story's beginning, remaining in the dark with respect to its middle and end.

No.

You have a general sense of what's happening during your story's beginning, middle, *and* end. This makes writing your rough draft less daunting and infinitely more manageable.

Even if you get stuck, the moment is likely to pass quickly, because you won't be traversing in the dark, where you don't know what happens next, for very long.

You'll have a bearing to head toward, a destination just around the corner. Should you need it, this knowledge will rekindle your enthusiasm to finish your draft.

Hence, you're unlikely to become so discouraged that you abandon your project altogether—the tragic result that frequently arises when you write blindly from FADE IN or Chapter 1.

If you're a pantser, figuring out the structure of your story is enough to (a) stave off overwhelm so you actually finish your draft, and (b) avoid the monumental work of building structure into it, after the fact.

At the same time, you probably won't feel like your creativity is being stifled by the imposition of story structure. The in-betweens—the events in between your structural signposts—are still unknown elements, enabling your imagination to fly free, without added constraints.

However, if you're a plotter like me, you need more. To write with confidence and to maximize your productivity, you need more than a general sense of how your story unfolds. You need to know what happens next—not periodically, but at all times.

You need a full outline, a list of all the plot points that comprise your screenplay or novel.

Once more, story structure comes to the rescue. It's the key step to take you from logline to outline. See, after you've figured out the structure of your story, figuring out the in-betweens is child's play.

Think of it like (new metaphor alert!) cracking the combination, or code, to a safe. Once all the numbers in the code have been deduced, the tumblers fall into place, and the safe door opens, revealing the treasures inside.

Similarly, when you determine your story's essential plot points, when you crack its structural code, your story will open up, gaining you access to the remaining plot points that will spill out like little gold nuggets.

Once you have those nuggets—hey, presto!—your outline will be complete, and you can tell the blank page, "You don't scare me anymore." Filled with the confidence of always knowing what happens next, you will be fired up to write your rough draft.

But I'm getting ahead of myself. First, whether plotter or pantser, you have to crack that code. To do so, it helps to have a solid understanding of its constituents—the topic of the following chapter.

To hear those tumblers go click, click, click as they unlock the structure of your story, continue reading!

- chapter eight -

AN OVERVIEW OF STORY STRUCTURE: THE 8 ESSENTIAL PLOT POINTS OF YOUR STORY OUTLINE

IN THIS CHAPTER, WE'LL COVER DEFINITIONS FOR THE eight essential plot points that constitute story structure.

Before we get into the definitions, it helps to know what these plot points are, exactly. Here's a list:

- opening and closing images
- inciting incident
- first-act break
- midpoint
- fork in the road
- trough of hell
- climax
- resolution

With that sorted, let's take a closer look at story structure…

(1) Opening and Closing Images

The opening image is audiences' initial introduction to your story.

Okay, technically, in some cases, audiences have already been introduced to your story through a movie trailer or a book cover or someone else's raving review (don't we all wish?).

Nevertheless, the opening image is audiences' first *real* introduction to your screenplay or novel, outside of marketing materials or word of mouth. A strong one is like an ambassador of sorts. It represents everything audiences are about to experience.

If you're writing a screenplay, beginning with an image is the norm. If you're writing a novel, you may lead with a line of dialogue, rather than with an image. Ideally, an image that encapsulates your story as a whole will make an appearance soon thereafter, within the first scene or chapter.

My favorite example of an opening image is from *The Fellowship of the Ring*. It starts with a picture of a smoldering crucible, which is a nifty container to melt metal in.

Since Frodo's goal is to destroy the One Ring, and turn it into molten metal again, this image really does say a thousand words. (Or, more accurately, based on the word count of Tolkien's trilogy, it says 450,000+ words.)

Similar to opening images, closing images embody your story's essence. Oftentimes, they are the visual answer to the question, *Why does this story matter?*

They're also audiences' final experience with your story, so choose well. Be sure to give audiences a proper send-off.

If you're feeling particularly bold, clever, or devious, you may select a closing image that casts your story in a new light and causes audiences to re-evaluate a fair portion of what they've just read or watched. The spinning top in *Inception* is a good example.

I have to admit, originally, I didn't put much stock into opening and closing images, until Blake Snyder's book *Save the Cat* convinced me of their value.

(2) Inciting Incident

This is the event (or a combination of them) that gets your story started. It changes the dynamics of your protagonist's life.

If the inciting incident didn't happen, life would pretty much go on as usual for your protagonist. He would not pursue his SMART goal. He'd never go on the journey you have planned for him. (By the way, when I say *journey*, I don't just mean a physical journey, but let's save that discussion for the next key plot point, the first-act break.)

Mostly any event can work as an inciting incident. That said, the same inciting incident crops up repeatedly in certain genres.

In action movies, thrillers, and mysteries, the protagonist is often assigned to a case. In romances, the hero and heroine meet for the first time.

Of course, you can make your thriller or romance stand out by putting a fresh twist on these conventions.

(3) First-Act Break

As the invisible boundary between the last scene of Act One and the first scene of Act Two, the first-act break is where your story really takes off.

Throughout Act One, you laid down groundwork for audiences to (a) understand and (b) care about later events. Now, at the first-act break, it's time for your protagonist to launch his plans; it's time for him to take active steps to achieve his goal.

In short, it's the beginning of your protagonist's journey.

Oftentimes, the first-act break will be marked by a change in geographical location, like when the Dashwood family relocates to Barton Park in *Sense and Sensibility* (1995), or when Bond goes to the Bahamas to stir up mayhem (but no martinis) in *Casino Royale* (2006).

However, your protagonist doesn't have to travel to new locations to go on a journey. His adventure may be more overtly psychological or spiritual in nature.

In *It's Complicated*, for instance, Jane is by no means stationary. But she doesn't go on a physical journey per se. Instead, when she becomes her ex-husband's mistress, she explores new psychological terrain, experiencing life as the woman Jack is cheating *with*, rather than *on*.

(4) Midpoint

As its name implies, the midpoint clocks in about halfway

through your story. Basically, it's a fulcrum that swings your story in a new direction.

As a result, the vast expanse of your story middle doesn't become monotonous, and audiences don't get bored and tune out. That's the goal, anyway.

We'll discuss the midpoint in much greater detail in chapter 11, where I'll show you how your logline (created in action step #12) can instantly guide you toward a suitable midpoint fulcrum.

(5) Fork in the Road

At this stage of your story, your protagonist is at a crossroad and must make a choice about how to proceed. Although he's made several decisions before reaching this point, this particular choice feels momentous in some way.

Maybe because it's especially daring or controversial. Maybe because it's a reversal of an earlier decision or attitude, one that the protagonist seemed unlikely to abandon. (In fact, this is a great way to show character growth.)

Maybe because it's the wrong choice.

Notice that *wrong* has multiple shadings in meaning; it all depends on context. A choice can be wrong because:

- It will hurt your protagonist's chances of achieving his current goal.
- It will hurt other protagonists' chances of achieving their goals.

- It takes your protagonist closer to achieving a goal that he actually needs to reject (i.e. the *want* in want-vs.-need stories).

- It takes your protagonist closer to achieving his goal, but via means he's not keen to implement.

- Audiences are rooting against it!

Here are a couple of genre-based ways the fork may play out: in a thriller, the protagonist might choose to commit to the case he's spent significant time trying to weasel out of. In a romance with a love triangle, the hero may walk away from the heroine, opting instead to be with the heroine's competition.

While the fork in the road comes after the midpoint in our list of essential plot points, its placement is quite flexible. It can occur before, after, or even coincide with, the midpoint.

Note: The fork in the road often involves an escalation of commitment by the protagonist. Without going into excessive detail, I want to acknowledge that it's inspired by Viki King's "point of commitment," as described in her screenwriting guide, *How to Write a Movie in 21 Days*.

(6) Trough of Hell

The trough of hell marks the end of Act Two, when it *seems* like your protagonist is the furthest away from his goal. It goes by other names, such as the "all is lost" or black moment.

I refer to this plot point as the trough of hell as a reminder that this is not the time to use kid gloves; it's the time to inflict as much damage onto your protagonist as possible.

Why?

The emotional intensity of this painful experience will re-engage audiences, right when their attention has the tendency to wane. That's why the trough of hell, coupled with the midpoint, will prevent the middle of your story from sagging.

Did you notice that I put "seems" in italics in the first paragraph describing the trough? I did that because the trough, quite paradoxically, brings the protagonist *closer* to his objective, even though, on the surface, he appears to be the furthest from it.

For instance, the trough may bring the protagonist into contact with a vital resource or key intel that he needs to vanquish the villain. Or, the protagonist's painful experience may force him to employ a strategy he'd prefer to avoid—but which he must embrace, in order to succeed.

(7) Climax

The climax is the final showdown between your protagonist and his central antagonist. (If you're writing a series, it's the final showdown within this particular series installment.)

Since audiences started reading your story, they've wondered whether your protagonist will get what he wants. Because audiences may operate on the assumption that most stories end happily, perhaps it's better to rephrase: they wonder *how* your protagonist will get what he wants.

Either way, the climax provides audiences with the answer, showing them the steps the protagonist takes in order to settle matters with the antagonist once and for all.

In *Gladiator*, audiences wonder whether Maximus will avenge his family, and, to a lesser extent, whether Rome will become a republic. When Maximus slays the emperor during their final confrontation in the Colosseum, both these questions are answered.

(8) Resolution

The resolution emerges from the outcome of the climax. Resolutions can be brief or extended.

In an extended happy ending, audiences get to see—in detail—the protagonist enjoying the fruits of his labor. Although not as prolonged, brief resolutions (in stories that end happily) still manage to strike a high note.

Of course, your story may not end happily, but tragically. Your protagonist may fail to achieve his goal. The choice is yours. Bear in mind, however, that happy endings generally have more commercial appeal.

To achieve a compromise, consider tempering your tragic ending with an undercurrent of positivity, so that it becomes less tragic and more bittersweet.

• • •

Story structure has probably given you a headache in the past. Hopefully, this overview has made it less impenetrable and easier to fathom. Nevertheless, there's more work to be done.

Even though you're now well versed in story structure, we have yet to discuss how you can apply this knowledge and crack the structural code of *your own* story.

That's what we'll cover in the next six chapters. Before we dive in, there is one little wrinkle that should be mentioned. We're not going to discuss the plot points in order, the way they were described in this chapter (and the way they'll probably appear in your story).

Instead, we're going to deviate (slightly) and cover them in the order that makes the most sense for you, as a writer, to figure each one out.

To get started, turn the page!

- chapter nine -

TAKING YOUR STORY OFF THE GROUND VIA THE FIRST-ACT BREAK

To describe the first-act break, many metaphors come to mind.

It can be when:

- The training wheels come off of your story.
- Your story pulls away from the train station and heads off toward its next destination.
- Your story taxis down an airport runway and lifts off. (According to Chris Vogler's *The Writer's Journey*, this metaphor is used at Disney.)
- Your story takes off, like a racehorse flying out of the starting gate when a race begins.
- All your chess pieces are in place, and now it's time to play.

Did you notice that these metaphors all share something in common?

They all have to do with motion.

Therein lies the key to figuring out the first-act break. It's simply your logline "in motion," the point where it springs into action.

Whatever the logline says, that's basically the essence of the first-act break. It's where most (if not all) components of the logline coalesce. Because the logline encapsulates the hook, by default, the first-act break is where the main intrinsic hook of a story will manifest itself as well.

There is one major exception to this, which we'll discuss later on. But for the most part, figuring out the first-act break really is that easy. By condensing your idea into a logline, you've actually taken a huge step in cracking your story's structural code.

Let's say that your hook is about a middle-aged divorcé who poses as an elderly female nanny in order to spend more time with his children. The first-act break is where that would happen—and this is indeed where Daniel Hillard emerges as the eponymous *Mrs. Doubtfire*.

Here's another one: the hook is about a teenager who travels back in time to the day when his parents first met. When does this happen in *Back to the Future*?

Not in the first 10 minutes.

Nope.

It happens at the first-act break, 31 minutes into the movie.

One final example, this time from one of the loglines from chapter 7. To review, a potential logline for *The Proposal* could be:

To avoid deportation, a high-maintenance New York editor fakes an engagement to the assistant who despises her, and must convince his family (who resides in Sitka, Alaska) that their romance is real.

When is the fish (the New York editor) thrown into new waters (Sitka)? Take a guess!

Right at the first-act break. (Notice the change in geographical location, a common feature of the first-act break.)

So easy, so painless…and kind of obvious as well, at least in retrospect.

But when I first had this realization, it was a real lightbulb moment for me, which significantly reduced my panic over how to structure my story. If you're having trouble with the first-act break, I hope this insight will lead to an aha moment for you, too.

Then, when I, all pleased as punch, got my first-act break sorted, I had another epiphany. Figuring out how the first act ended wasn't the real problem at all. Knowing what to fill it with—now, that's the hard part.

Beginners (as well as more experienced writers, who, for whatever reason, are feeling insecure about their project) often stuff their first act with too much. This error leads to reviews like, "This story starts off real slow."

Of course, some reviewers might follow that up with a comment like, "Despite taking awhile to get started, it got so much better. I'm glad I kept reading!"

Such positive comments can give you false hope and convince you that you can bypass the unwelcome task of scaling back your story's beginning. But this outcome occurs due to sheer luck; it's not a reaction you should bank on, especially if you're trying to build your career.

If you're not a known commodity, if your readers don't know you have a track record of spinning straw into gold, then they're probably not going to give you the benefit of the doubt.

More than likely, they'll put down your screenplay or novel, and replace it with one that isn't bogged down by too much exposition or too many mini-flashbacks at its beginning.

Instead of overstuffing your first act, dole out details the way the military does: on a "need to know" basis.

To figure out what qualifies, here are five questions to consider:

- What do audiences need to know now to understand what happens immediately after the first-act break?
- What do audiences need to know to understand events long after the first-act break, when audiences are deep in the middle of your story, but which you need to reveal now to maintain momentum and pacing later on?
- What do audiences need to know to be properly oriented with your story? (Details about setting, genre, and tone would fit the bill.)

- What do audiences need to know now so that they'll believe later events?
- What do audiences need to know now so that they'll be emotionally connected to what happens later on?

Bear in mind, it's possible to err in the other direction. From a movie trailer or a book's cover copy, audiences know what your hook is. That's what got them to choose your story in the first place.

Since you know audiences are expecting this hook, you may rush to provide it, putting your logline in motion too early. If you had written *Back to the Future*, for instance, you might've sent Marty back in time, to the year 1955, within the first 10 pages of your script.

Even though it may feel counterintuitive to delay presenting the hook in full, you can't rush it. Mostly because of the last item on our need-to-know list of questions.

In order for audiences to care about what happens after the first act (during Acts Two and Three), they need to spend quality time with your protagonist.

Not later, but now.

They'll also need to spend time with the stakes (although, this can sometimes be delayed until the beginning of Act Two).

This line from J. J. Abrams's "Mystery Box" TED Talk sums it up best: "There's a half an hour of investment in character before you get to the stuff that you're, you know, expecting." [6]

Half an hour. Where did this number come from?

In a movie with a 2-hour running time, half an hour equates to 25% of the story. Generally speaking, that's the magic number that will help you keep your first act on track.

If the first act runs shorter (down to 10%, let's say), then audiences are probably not going to care about what happens later on, even if it's really exciting.

Conversely, if the first act runs over (consuming 30% of your story, for instance), then audiences may feel like you've taken too long to get your story off the ground. Brimming with impatience, they're likely to abandon your story before they ever reach the exciting stuff you have in store for them.

That said, there is some leeway here. In a science-fiction story that requires tons of worldbuilding, the first act may run longer than 25%. In novels, 20% may be sufficient. In a comedy script, even less.

Use your best judgment. Justify your choices.

Always, always ask yourself, *Does my audience need to know this?*

ACTION STEP(S)

(13) Determine the first-act break of your story.

Revisit your logline from action step #12. Select an event, or a combination of them, that expresses your logline in motion.

Here's another way to look at it: you're taking the main hook of your story, the "wow" element from your concept, and putting it into a story event.

(14) Figure out what goes onto your need-to-know list.

Make a quick list of what audiences need to know now in order to understand or care about what happens at, and after, the first-act break.

You might not have a clear idea of what happens after the first-act break. In fact, that's pretty common. Don't worry about it. Fill in what you can. Focus on what you need to explain for audiences to buy into the hook. For instance, in *Mrs. Doubtfire*, you'd have to explain how Daniel could get ahold of the makeup and prosthetics necessary to transform him into an elderly woman.

Set your list aside, just as you did with your story seeds.

If you try to squeeze all of these details into your story right off the bat, you'll likely feel overwhelmed. A better strategy is to outline your story first (using the method discussed in Part III of this book, or another method of your choice), or, if you prefer, finish your rough draft. Afterward, assess the beginning of your outline (or rough draft) and double-check that you've covered everything on your need-to-know list.

By the time you reach this point, some of the items on your list might not be relevant anymore, and you can simply cross them off. And if you've missed something, you can now weave it organically into your story.

- chapter ten -

BEGINNING WITH A BANG VIA THE INCITING INCIDENT AND THE OPENING IMAGE

ONCE YOU'VE FIGURED OUT YOUR FIRST-ACT BREAK, you should have little trouble with the inciting incident.

See, the two are causally linked. The inciting incident, whatever it is, enables your logline to spring into motion.

It's the event that compels your protagonist, at this juncture in his life, to go on his journey, launch his outlandish scheme, and pursue his SMART goal.

Accordingly, to figure out the inciting incident, you just need to work backward. Start with the first-act break, and then think of something—anything—that could cause it to happen.

And voila! Instant inciting incident.

Yep. Just like that.

Anything works, just as long as you can connect the inciting incident to the first-act break via cause and effect.

To illustrate, let's revisit our ironic mayoral election campaign from chapter 6. Our heroine is a single mother, who happens to fall in love with her main political rival.

To determine an inciting incident for our story, all we have to do is find a way to embroil her in the mayoral race. Naturally, we'll have to find a way to bring in her political rival. But we can take care of that later. Involving her is enough to kickstart our story.

As you may recall, pot holes (of all things) served as the impetus behind our heroine's SMART goal. It can serve as the foundation of our inciting incident too. En route to her daughter's school, the heroine swerves to avoid a pot hole, and ends up in a minor accident.

Having chalked up another tardy, her daughter gets detention. Our heroine, meanwhile, gets a humiliating dressing-down from the school's principal. Fuming, the heroine concludes, *This whole situation could've been prevented, if only that pot hole had been repaired on time as our mayor promised…*

…and the rest of the first act unfolds from there.

That wasn't hard, was it? Indeed, cracking your structural code has been pretty easy so far. You've already got two essential plot points, in hand, ready to go. And it only took about 10 minutes to figure them out, probably less.

Awesome, no?

With this feeling in mind, let's forge ahead, onto the opening image. I've gotta be frank. Even when you know the entire plot of your story, picking the opening image isn't easy.

Currently, you only know two plot points. That's meaningful progress sure, but it's probably not enough to select a decent image, let alone one that perfectly encapsulates your story.

So, for practical purposes, we're going to broaden the definition of the opening image. Think of it as a picture of your protagonist's everyday life, right before the inciting incident comes along and disrupts everything.

Right before.

Hmmm. That's a bit vague, isn't it? How far back in time do you go?

Below are a few options:

- Start 1 hour before the inciting incident occurs.
- Start 24 hours before the inciting incident occurs.
- Start immediately after the inciting incident occurs. (Yes, that's after, not before, but it's equally viable.)

You may've noticed that all of these options occur fairly close in time to the inciting incident. Many stories actually start further away, maybe with a prologue that happens long before the main plot begins.

All the same, I suggest you begin your outline closer in time to the inciting incident. This minimizes the chances that you'll fill your first act with too much unnecessary information that audiences, quite simply, do not need to know.

Later on, when you've completed your outline, you may decide to change your opening, maybe morph it into a prologue. As a matter of fact, the inciting incident in the final draft of your story may deviate from the event you choose now.

Truth be told, it doesn't really matter what you select for the inciting incident and opening image. Not at this point.

Here's why: you're just trying to find a way into your outline, and by extension, your story. What do I mean by *finding a way in*? When you find your way inside, you can easily generate plenty of raw material.

Some of it—maybe even the majority of it—may go, but (glory be!), you've got stuff to work with. Stuff you didn't have before, when you were trying to find your way in.

To clarify, let's pick a new metaphor. Finding a way into your story is like infiltrating the interior of a castle. You've got plenty of approaches to choose from.

You could:

- catapult yourself over the ramparts (as Robin Hood and Azeem do in *Prince of Thieves*)
- scale the walls with grapple-hook ladders (as Saruman's army does in *The Two Towers*)
- destroy the gate with a battering ram (as William Wallace and his Scottish army do in *Braveheart*)
- sneak in via the sewers (as the dwarves do in *Snow White & the Huntsman*)
- ensconce yourself inside a gift that is then brought into the castle interior (the way Odysseus, Achilles, and the Greeks do to infiltrate *Troy*)

- access the interior through a secret underground passage (a movie example escapes my mind)

As leader of the men trying to infiltrate a castle, you may first select the battering-ram approach. It may work; it may fail. In the case of the latter, you'll have to re-evaluate your strategy and opt for something else.

Even if it's successful (assuming you have to infiltrate a similar castle), you may select another strategy in the future. That's because, once you got inside the castle via the battering ram, you acquired new insight. You realized that sneaking in via the sewers would've been more efficient.

Nevertheless, using the battering ram wasn't a total loss.

It did, after all, get you in!

And *that*'s what counts.

Let's bring things back to storytelling. The inciting incident and opening image you select at this point may stay the same, from now through your final daft. That's great. On the other hand, they may be more akin to the battering ram in our analogy.

They get you into your story, generating tons of raw material. The raw material, in turn, gains you more insight, ultimately leading you toward a superior alternative for your inciting incident or opening image (this is the equivalent of the sneaky sewer attack in our castle analogy).

The point is this: the first approach you take may be perfect for the story you're trying to tell. It may not be. Even if it's not, more than likely, it will lead you to something that *is*.

Since you've got to start somewhere, you have to select an inciting incident and opening image now—with the understanding that they may change later on. (FYI: The first act, in general, tends to undergo a lot of reshuffling.)

ACTION STEP(S)

(15) Choose an inciting incident for your story.

Reflect on the first-act break you designed in action step #13. Pick something—anything—that could logically lead to this set of events. That's your inciting incident.

Remember, you're not committing to it now; it could change.

You're just generating fodder for your imagination, so it can, in turn, generate sufficient raw material for you (at a later point) to accurately gauge what belongs in the final product—and what doesn't.

(16) Find your opening image, i.e. your point of entry into your story.

Before the inciting incident comes along, disrupts everything, and embroils your protagonist in the plot, what was your protagonist doing?

The inciting incident you chose in action step #15, along with your story's ironic hook, should give you a clue and imply a starting position, or the "status quo," for your protagonist.

Taking no more than 20 minutes, describe (a) what your

protagonist was doing 0–24 hours before the inciting incident and (b) what he does 0–24 hours after it. Write at least half a page for each.

Based on what you've written, determine whether you want to begin your story before or after the inciting incident takes place.

Finally, isolate a moment from the time period you've chosen (i.e. before or after). Use this moment as your point of entry into your story.

- chapter eleven -

SWINGING YOUR STORY IN A NEW DIRECTION VIA THE MIDPOINT

LET'S START WITH SOME PRELIMINARIES: THE midpoint neatly divides the middle (or Act Two) of your story into two parts of roughly equal length.

In screenwriting parlance, the first half of the second act is commonly referred to as Act 2A, while the latter half is commonly referred to as Act 2B. As explained in chapter 8, ideally, the midpoint isn't just a divider. It's also a fulcrum that swings your story in a new direction.

In other words, the events that populate Act 2B should differ in some key respect to the events that populate Act 2A. Because Act 2B isn't the same as Act 2A, the middle of your story shouldn't feel monotonous.

Cracking this particular number in your structural code has

probably caused you a lot of consternation in the past. It's about to get easier—and you don't need any fancy safecracking equipment either. Just your logline and this book.

See, the premises of most stories naturally lend themselves to specific kinds of fulcrums. From action step #12, you already know your premise.

Now you just need to know what kind of fulcrum it, like a jigsaw puzzle piece, tends to go with—and I'm about to share eight fulcrum types with you.

You ready? Let's go!

8 Ways to Swing Your Story in a New Direction

Below is a handy list of eight midpoint fulcrums, which can be readily deployed to swing the middle of your screenplay or novel in a new direction:

(1) Bond Builder

With this fulcrum, the premise involves characters (usually two) who are hostile toward each other, or, if not hostile, reluctant to embrace their coexistence (often coerced).

At the midpoint, they share a moment of emotional or physical intimacy (or both), and form a bond whose creation swings the story in a new direction.

Although a go-to choice for romances, this fulcrum can also be applied to platonic partnerships, such as that between professional colleagues or a coach and his sports team.

(2) BFF Breaker

This fulcrum is the polar opposite of the bond builder. Here, the bond between the characters (again, usually two) is well established. However, something (often the hook) tests this relationship.

At the midpoint, the cracks start to show, gradually escalating until the relationship breaks.

Note: Although I've used the acronym BFF (Best Friends Forever) to dub this fulcrum, it can be applied to any interpersonal relationship, not just friendship.

(3) Tide Turner

With this midpoint fulcrum, the tides can swing in either direction (positive or negative). It depends on the nature of your premise.

During Act 2A, your protagonist could endure a prolonged series of failures—until the midpoint, when he finally tastes a meaningful bite of success. (This works very well for fish-out-of-water concepts, especially when they're built on the difference between your protagonist's field of competency and his predicament.)

Alternatively, your protagonist may enjoy one "high" after another—until the midpoint, when he starts to realize that all of this fun is meaningless (or loaded with drawbacks). This variation of the tide-turner fulcrum is often employed in wish-fulfillment stories.

If you use the tide-turner midpoint, bear in mind that each half, whether positive or negative, doesn't have to be uniform.

That is to say, although Act 2A may be overwhelmingly filled with failure, a few successes may be sprinkled in between (and vice versa). Likewise, although the majority of Act 2B may lean toward success, failure might not be altogether absent (and vice versa).

As a matter of fact, Act 2B will probably culminate in a massive failure—the trough of the story. We'll cover the trough in greater depth in due course. But for now, let's move on to the next midpoint type, the—

(4) Passivity Pivot

"On the run" plots lend themselves to this fulcrum, where the protagonist transitions from being passive (or reactive) to being active (or proactive) at the midpoint.

During Act 2A, the protagonist is presented as the hunted, not the hunter. This is a defensive stance. It's inherently passive.

But at the midpoint, the protagonist will change his strategy and become less reactive. Going on the offensive during Act 2B, he'll pursue an agenda that encompasses more than just eluding capture.

(5) Antagonist Aha

This midpoint fulcrum is most often associated with action movies, thrillers, and mysteries in which the protagonist is (or behaves like) a sleuth. During Act 2A, although he searches for clues and chases down leads and conducts interrogations, his actions are rather haphazard.

At the midpoint, however, he experiences an aha moment, and gains greater understanding into his antagonist. Specifically, the sleuth learns more about the antagonist's identity, nature, or end game.

Hence, during Act 2B, although the sleuth is still searching for clues, etc., his focus usually becomes narrower, and his actions more targeted, as he concentrates on a smaller pool of elements.

This fulcrum can also be used in romances. The heroine, for example, may gain greater insight into the hero, or perhaps, the wrong suitor. But if you're writing a romance, it's probably going to be more helpful to view your fulcrum as a bond builder (previously discussed) or a revelation acceleration (up next!).

(6) Revelation Acceleration

The revelation acceleration is very similar to the antagonist-aha fulcrum in that the protagonist usually gains greater understanding into his antagonist. However, the revelation acceleration contains either an element of (a) surprise (b) dramatic irony or (c) both that is lacking from the antagonist-aha midpoint type.

In the case of surprise, the writer will make a shocking reveal at the midpoint that will compel audiences to re-evaluate everything they've just read or watched (e.g. the protagonist's best bud is the villain).

In the case of dramatic irony, audiences are already clued in to the reveal. At the midpoint, one (or more) of the characters learns the secret (e.g. the protagonist is perpetrating a ruse that audiences have known about from the beginning, and now, another character is in the loop).

Okay, those descriptions explain the revelation aspect of this midpoint. What about the acceleration aspect?

Well, these are the kinds of reveals that writers often delay making until the end of Act Two. With this fulcrum, these reveals are moved up to the middle of your story (around the 50%-mark). That's why they're accelerated—you're hastening their disclosure.

(7) Manifest Midpoint

Remember when we were talking about the first-act break? I said it is—with one exception—when the logline springs into motion.

This is it. The exception, I mean. With some stories, it's fair to say that the logline (and hence the hook) only manifest themselves in full at the midpoint.

Until then, audiences experience the "lite" or "shadow" version of the concept. During Act 2B, audiences experience the "substance" or the full manifestation of the hook.

By the way, with respect to the manifest midpoint, we're not talking about tone- or title-based hooks, etc. We're talking about the hooks that arise from your story's (often ironic) premise.

This fulcrum is a tricky one to grasp, so let's look at a specific example, *The Hunger Games*. A possible logline for the story could be: a teenage girl must fight other teenagers—till the death—in a televised reality show ordained by the government.

To truly deliver on the hook, for it to really manifest in full, the teenage girl (Katniss) has to be *in the arena*, fighting off her competition. That doesn't happen in the movie.

At least, it doesn't happen as part of Act 2A. It occurs *after* the midpoint. Till then, audiences watch as Katniss prepares for the Games. This is the shadow version of the concept.

(8) Game Changer

I'll say it straight out: this midpoint fulcrum is just convenient shorthand to describe midpoints where it's clear that the story is swinging in a new direction, but the other seven midpoint types don't accurately categorize the shift. (That sure is a mouthful, isn't it? Which is why the shorthand is…well, so handy.)

For instance, this might work as a game changer: at the midpoint, the character you've presented as the hero transitions into the villain, while the character originally portrayed as the villain takes on the role of the hero.

As a stickler for precision, I should add that the transition has to be portrayed gradually to be a game changer. If it's abrupt, then it's probably more accurate to classify the fulcrum as a revelation acceleration.

Is this distinction meaningful? Only to the extent that it helps you organize your thoughts regarding the way you want to develop the middle of your story.

Matching Your Premise with the Perfect Midpoint

With this system, picking a midpoint for your story should be a breeze. You just have to match your logline with one of the eight midpoint fulcrums.

To demonstrate how easy the process is, I'm going to use *Mrs. Doubtfire* as an example. Before we begin, I want to stress that I'm working only from the logline (and two character names: Daniel and Mrs. Doubtfire), not the movie.

These midpoint fulcrums may appear, in one form or another, in the film; they may not. It doesn't really matter because this is just an intellectual exercise to show you how to make the midpoint-fulcrum system work for you.

The first part of the process is to examine your logline from action step #12 and see if any fulcrums immediately jump out. Usually one or two will.

Here's a possible logline for *Mrs. Doubtfire*: when the ex-wife of a middle-aged male voiceover artist minimizes his contact with their children, he poses as an elderly female nanny in order to spend more time with them.

When I look at this logline, two fulcrums immediately spring to my mind. One is the tide turner. In regard to physical appearance and comportment, it's not going to be easy for a middle-aged man (i.e. Daniel) to pretend that he's an elderly female (i.e. Mrs. Doubtfire). He's going to have trouble walking in her shoes, to put it mildly.

Accordingly, Act 2A could be filled with several failed attempts to get it right. But then, at the midpoint, Daniel could succeed. In fact, his success could be so massive that his wife could ask him (as Mrs. Doubtfire) to move into their house, as a live-in nanny. This situation would make things even dicier for Daniel, as it'd be more difficult to keep the ruse going.

Speaking of ruses, they're always a prime candidate for the revelation-acceleration fulcrum. That's the second option that leaps out as a possibility. Daniel's ruse could be exposed here, at the midpoint, instead of at the end of Act Two (or at the climax).

To whom is Daniel's fraud going to be exposed? It doesn't have to be to everyone—just one meaningful character will do.

To answer this question, it helps to quickly list all the characters who are designated or implied by the logline. This is what my list looks like:

- Daniel
- Daniel's alter ego, Mrs. Doubtfire
- Daniel's children
- Daniel's ex-wife
- someone who helps Daniel transform into Mrs. Doubtfire (assuming Daniel can't do the whole thing himself, the presence of such an individual is implied by the logline)

Now, with this list, answers become readily apparent. Daniel's deceit could be exposed to his children or to his ex-wife. Frankly, I don't see a way for the latter option to work.

Once Daniel's deceit is exposed to his ex-wife, it's kind of game over for the plot. I'm going to reject this possibility right off the bat, but I'm going to include "double life exposed to children" as a potential midpoint.

We've got two viable midpoints (the tide turner and the revelation acceleration) in less than 5 minutes! Very, very cool.

But let's not stop there. Let's see if there are other, less obvious options that have been overlooked so far.

When it's time for you to do this on your own, first re-examine your master list of midpoint fulcrums. Then, tailor them to your story by connecting them to the characters on the list you just jotted down. Put another way, you'll be creating a dynamic between your characters that matches the essence of a midpoint you've yet to take for a test-drive.

Returning to our *Mrs. Doubtfire* hypothetical, I'm going to see if I can make it work with the bond builder. Between whom can I build a bond?

I suppose Daniel could share a moment with his ex-wife at the midpoint. Maybe he could realize that she's not the shrew he thinks she is, and he really is the one with the attitude problem. This could be one of those stories where the estranged couple gets back together at the end.

While that's certainly a serviceable option, when I play around with my list of characters, a more interesting possibility emerges. What if I build a bond not between Daniel and his ex-wife, but between Mrs. Doubtfire and Daniel's ex-wife?

Even though this take on the bond-builder fulcrum is different than the one preceding it, because Daniel and Mrs. Doubtfire are one and the same, it can yield an identical result—Daniel realizes his ex-wife is not a shrew; maybe they get back together. Even if they don't, Daniel's realization could be a good way to integrate character growth into this farce. Excellent.

Having decided that the bond builder makes the grade, I'm going to test out another fulcrum. Actually, I'm going to test out its opposite, the BFF breaker. Can I make it work too?

Yep, sure can.

Daniel can't be at two different places at the same time. It makes sense that the more he comes to his family's rescue as Mrs. Doubtfire, the more he's going to disappoint them as Daniel. Thus, during Act 2A, his kids could be willing to give him the benefit of the doubt, but after a major disappointment at the midpoint, they might begin to withdraw emotionally from him.

Here's another variation of the BFF breaker: the friend who helped Daniel with his transformation could become fed up with Daniel's deceit and accuse Daniel of taking the ruse too far. Maybe this friend could be secretly in love with Daniel's ex-wife, which would certainly complicate things.

Regardless, at the midpoint, the cracks in his friendship with Daniel could start to show, especially if the friend withdraws his assistance, and Daniel has to transform into Mrs. D on his own.

To be honest, although I like the idea of Daniel fending for himself, without his friend's help, I'm not very keen on this variation of the BFF-breaker fulcrum. I don't think it's strong enough to anchor the middle of the story. But I'm not going to reject it out of hand. You never know, it might become useful subplot material later on.

There's one more possibility to explore: the manifest midpoint. The hook of the film is seeing Daniel deal with life as Mrs. Doubtfire. Theoretically, I could delay his transformation into the elderly nanny until the midpoint.

But if I do that, what am I going to do for Act 2A, the shadow version of the concept? I have absolutely no clue. I'm going to discard this option for now…and revisit it later, after I've finished my outline.

Then, I'll know more about the story and my characters. I may be able to think of a suitable shadow version of the concept, something that can entertain audiences until my hook fully manifests itself. If I wish, I can modify my outline and incorporate the shadow version into it.

You might be wondering why I'd even bother to do this. It may seem like a lot of unnecessary work. It would be—if my story escalates nicely. But if, in my outline, my story doesn't escalate very well, then the manifest midpoint could be the perfect way to solve the problem.

Okay, I'm going to stop here. I'm not going to explore the three remaining midpoint fulcrums: the antagonist aha, the passivity pivot, and the game changer. Mostly because I don't think this premise lends itself to any of these fulcrums, and I'm not going to force it.

Without them, I've got plenty to work with…

How to Handle Multiple Midpoint Fulcrums

Many times, you're going to be in the same boat. You're going to discover that your premise lends itself to multiple midpoint fulcrums.

By *multiple*, I'm talking about two circumstances: (1) you have multiple midpoints that you can use *in isolation* (re: *Mrs. Doubtfire*, assuming I could get the manifest midpoint to work, I could use it or the tide turner—but probably not both); or (2) you have multiple midpoints that you can use *in conjunction*, by weaving them together via cause and effect (I could easily combine the tide-turner fulcrum with the BFF breaker, specifically the variation with the rift between Daniel and his children).

When faced with this interesting dilemma, what should you do?

Pick one fulcrum.

Just one.

Choose the one that you feel will help you best flesh out your outline, the one you're most excited to work with.

But, you might be asking yourself, *why impose a limit?*

Juggling more than one at a time tends to be overwhelming. Unnecessary, too. When you complete your outline by focusing on one fulcrum, oftentimes, you'll find that the others (that can be used in conjunction with it) will be taken care of by default. And if they're not, there'll be ample opportunity to address that later.

If you're torn between two midpoints that simply cannot be woven together, commit to one now, and outline your story twice (once with the fulcrum you committed to; the second time with the other). I know that sounds like it's a bugbear. But if you don't generate two outlines, you'll probably question whether the fulcrum you chose is better than the one you rejected.

Back and forth, back and forth, back and forth you'll go, second-guessing yourself every step of the way. To avoid this mental exhaustion, you have to buck up and outline your story two times. Then you'll be able to compare both outlines and see which one you like better.

Plus, with the method I'll describe in Part III of this book, outlining your story—even two versions of it—should be fairly quick and painless. As a side note, if you embrace iterative outlining, you'll have to get used to this (generating multiple outlines, making comparisons); it's a key part of stage 2.

Before we move on to the action steps for this chapter, a quick observation: when you choose the midpoint fulcrum for your story, its shape will become more defined and less amorphous. This will either thrill you to no end…or make you extremely anxious (especially if you're not used to defining the trajectory of your story so early on in the writing process).

Remember your objective here. It's not to choose the story events that will *definitely* be part of the final product. It's to choose the events that will enable you to generate a starter outline that will give you greater insight into your story.

With this insight, you can revisit options you've discarded, and discover ways to incorporate them into your story—ways that you couldn't see before because you simply didn't know enough.

Having made these discoveries, you can decide if you actually want to use them. You might; you might not.

Regardless, there's no reason to stew over your decision now. No matter what midpoint option you select, you're always going to come out on top.

ACTION STEP(S)

(17) Choose a midpoint fulcrum for your story.

Using your logline as a base, match up your premise to the midpoint fulcrums described in this chapter.

Start with the fulcrums that leap out first. Then, move on to fulcrums that are less obvious. Find a way to connect them to your premise.

To do this, it helps to jot down a list of characters that are either described or implied by your logline. Also, make sure to keep a record of your thought process, just like I did in this chapter.

After you've compiled a list of possibilities, pick one of them—just one—and proceed with the next chapter.

- chapter twelve -

RE-ENGAGING AUDIENCE INTEREST VIA THE TROUGH

Ah, the end of the second act, a.k.a. the trough.

It's a quagmire, the place where audiences tend to get antsy, the place where they start to weigh their boredom against the time they've already invested in your story.

Should they cut their losses and put it down? Or should they press forward, on to the end?

Naturally, you want them to opt for the latter.

Even better, though?

Not to have audiences in this position at all.

That's what a great trough does. To prevent audiences from tuning out here, you must bestow this part of your story with enough intensity to force them to sit up, take notice, and re-engage with your screenplay or novel.

As described in chapter 8, "An Overview of Story Structure," creating this wake-up call for audiences frequently entails crafting a sequence that is:

- painful for your hero
- emotionally resonant for audiences
- paradoxical with respect to the plot

Tall order.

Trying to fulfill it has probably given you the most grief.

The most anxiety.

The most nightmares.

Good news! Those days are over.

I'm going to give you a "cheat sheet" that will make you downright giddy to tackle Act 2B. Okay, that may be a bit of an exaggeration.

Even so, by casting light on Act 2B, the murkiest of story waters, this list should lighten your authorial burden. When implemented with skill, each item on it unites pain, emotion, and paradox into a powerful Act Two ending.

Here they are: your master list of trough types!

Your Master List of Trough Types

At the end of Act Two, your protagonist could…

- be captured
- appear to die (he can't actually die; then—unless there's another protagonist to pick up the task—audiences won't have a point of view to experience the events of your story)
- be banished (from a loved one, from his team, from working on the case)
- have his secret identity revealed to his antagonist
- become alienated from a love interest or friend

…or, as an alternative, an ally of the protagonist (rather than the protagonist himself), could be:

- captured
- killed (notice that an ally can die without creating any point-of-view problems)
- banished
- revealed to be a traitor

Doesn't Act 2B feel easier to write already?

Instead of having no clue about how to end the second act, you've got multiple options to pick from.

Of course, you're not obligated to use the trough types listed above as your Act Two ending. Feel free to devise one of your own.

Actually, while we're on the topic, I should mention that one trough type has been omitted from the above master list: your protagonist could be stonewalled. In other words, he reaches a dead end, as if the Great Wall of China were erected between him and his goal.

For example, your hero could be searching for a valuable ancient scroll—and finds it at the end of Act Two—only to discover that it's a fake. Alternatively, it's the genuine article, but in the hero's haste to elude the villain, the scroll gets destroyed.

As you can see, the stonewall trough type is rather open-ended, lending itself to multiple interpretations. That's why I didn't include it on the master list. If you're floundering, it's too all-encompassing to be useful.

Determining an Appropriate Act Two Ending

How should you go about it? Determining a trough that's appropriate for your story, I mean.

In this step-by-step system, the process is very similar to the one you went through to pick your midpoint. There are some differences, however.

While you can use your logline as your base, and try to match it up with a trough, you can also work from your midpoint fulcrum or from genre. See if they naturally suggest a trough to you.

Examples of working from a fulcrum: the BFF breaker frequently results in a trough of alienation, while the passivity pivot in on-the-run stories indicates a capture trough type.

Examples of working from genre: in a romance, at the end of Act Two, boy inevitably loses girl—the social alienation trough type. Death (of an ally) and capture (of an ally or the protagonist) are two candidates that are instantly indicated in an action movie or thriller.

When picking a midpoint, it's generally not that helpful to force connections between your premise and fulcrums that are unlikely to work. (If you recall, I didn't try to make the antagonist aha, passivity pivot, or game changer work for *Mrs. Doubtfire*.)

When picking a trough, it's different. Here, it's advantageous to take another tack and force yourself to make less intuitive choices fit into the preexisting framework of your story—especially for those trough types where your initial reaction is to say, "There's *no* way that would work!"

Why is this advantageous?

Well, by working with less obvious trough candidates and purposely adapting them to your story, you'll discover viable possibilities—that may significantly enhance your concept or give you a clearer picture of the second act—but which you would've prematurely discounted, had you not forced yourself to take a look.

Plus, by generating multiple trough types, you can braid them together, so that Act 2B virtually starts writing itself. How amazing is that?

In addition, with multiple troughs, your second-act ending should have sufficient intensity to recharge audiences' engagement with your story.

Frankly, many writers shy away from making their troughs painful, or hellacious, enough.

And the results aren't pretty.

You end up with that antsy-audience problem that we talked about at the beginning of this chapter. Instead of being enthralled by your story, audiences are impatient for it to wrap up.

With all the benefits a great trough sequence can provide, it behooves us to take a closer look at the process of trough selection. Like I did with picking a midpoint, I'm going to run through it right now. But because the midpoint example was lengthy (and because the two processes are similar), I'm keeping this one short, just sticking to the highlights.

I'm also going to keep things generic, working without a logline, and only from the passivity-pivot midpoint fulcrum. (This way, you'll be able to see how flexible this process can be, and how it can work for any on-the-run story, no matter the specifics of the logline.)

As stated earlier, in an on-the-run story, this fulcrum naturally goes with a capture trough type. For the sake of illustration, let's go beyond this first inclination and try to pair this fulcrum with another option.

I'm going to pick the death of an ally because, at first glance, it seems almost impossible to use this as my second-act ending. At this point, I don't even have any allies on my roster of characters, just the protagonist and some kind of antagonistic force, probably a villain.

To tackle this problem, my thought pattern looks like this: in these kinds of stories, the protagonist goes on the offensive during Act 2B, usually by infiltrating a high-security location in order to obtain information that will exonerate him.

So far, so good. Information can be conveyed in different ways. It can be conveyed through an object, like a paper file, memory card, or flash drive. It can also be conveyed through a person.

Voila!

This is the ally who can die at the end of Act Two.

To make the death happen, I just have to bring in the villain. Despite the protagonist's best efforts (which will surely involve nifty action stunts, thereby fulfilling genre expectations), the villain kills whoever was supposed to have knowledge that could exonerate the protagonist.

To make things really dire for the protagonist (and thus much more interesting for audiences), it'd be good if I can link the capture trough type with this additional one (the death of the ally). Fortunately, that's easy to do. Presumably, law enforcers are pursuing the protagonist; that is why he's on the run. This is a great moment for them to arrive on the scene. While the villain makes a quick getaway, the protagonist gets caught—right after witnessing his one hope for exoneration going up in flames.

With very little effort, I have a much clearer idea of how Act 2B is going to play out. That's not all. I also have audiences in the palm of my hand. I've dug such a deep trough for my protagonist that audiences aren't going to tune out from the story out of sheer boredom.

Far from it.

Reeling from the protagonist's losses, audiences are going to be in suspense, wondering how he's going to dig himself out of this hole.

Fair warning: the death of a character won't automatically generate an emotional response with the intensity required to keep audience interest at peak levels. You have to work at it.

If you're interested, you can find specific tips on how to craft a trough that's emotionally resonant (as well as how to sidestep problem spots associated with each trough type) in my writing guide *Trough of Hell*.

When you test out different trough types and try to adapt them to your story, you may come up with a predicament so dire, it seems impossible to extricate your protagonist from it.

Don't dismiss this possibility out of hand just because it's difficult to work with.

You may miss out on the perfect way to juice up the second act of your screenplay or novel. By giving into your fear and using an easier (but less exciting) option, you may be relegating your story to second-rate status.

Before moving on, as usual, I want to draw your attention to the level of specificity you're aiming for. When you're evaluating possible trough types, don't sweat the details.

Don't worry about the exact mechanics of the trough, the *how* of it.

You might not know the source of the betrayal that drives your best-friend protagonists apart; just that they're alienated from each other.

You might not know who's going to capture your protagonist (remember, it doesn't have to be the villain!); just that he's going to be captured.

Going back to our protagonist-on-the-run example, I know very little. I have no idea what kind of high-security building it is. (Incidentally, it doesn't have to be a building. Maybe it's a boat.) I don't have a clue about what information the ally knows and how it will exonerate the protagonist. All I know is that I want the infiltration sequence to be awesome, exciting, and near impossible for the protagonist to pull off.

Connecting the dots will come later, when you're outlining your story in full. When the time comes, your imagination will rise to the occasion and fill in the missing pieces, taking you from the midpoint all the way through to the trough.

Plus, at that stage of the outlining process, you will have discovered more about your story. The material you generate for Act 2A, for example, may give you a clearer picture of how your trough unfolds during Act 2B.

In the best-case scenario, you'll come up with something that exceeds your expectations. This outcome justifies taking on the risk of the worst-case scenario: you come up with something that's neither terribly interesting, nor entirely credible.

Still, that's not really much of a gamble, because even with this worst-case situation, you have something to work with.

That's the benefit of iterative outlining. And it beats the blank page any day of the week (and twice on Sundays).

So. Are you ready to unleash hell on your hero?

ACTION STEP(S)

(18a) Pick an obvious candidate for your trough.

Based on what you know (the midpoint fulcrum, the genre of your story, etc.) pick a suitable trough type from the master list in this chapter.

Usually, you won't have to expend much effort to incorporate it into your story; it's obvious that it will fit.

Repeat the process with other obvious candidates, and then choose the one you like best. Set the others aside—for the time being. (Make sure you keep a record of the troughs you discarded.)

(18b) Work backward from a random trough.

Select a different, nonintuitive trough type; it doesn't matter which one. Find a way to fit it into the framework of your story. In a teen comedy, for example, capture could play out as detention, while banishment could manifest as expulsion from school.

Repeat the process for all the trough types you're inclined to reject out of hand. Again choose the one you like best, and discard (temporarily) the rest.

Consider replacing the trough type from action step #18a with this one, from action step #18b, or—even better—follow the next action step.

(18c) Combine trough types.

Find a way to connect the trough type from action step #18a to the one from action step #18b.

If you can't think of a way right now, don't sweat it. A connection may reveal itself when you finish your outline. If you can only connect the troughs by resorting to outlandish or insipid means that have no business being in a final draft, that's okay too.

The important thing is that you're cultivating the habit of looking for multiple ways to put your protagonist through hell.

- chapter thirteen -

PUTTING THE "GRAND" IN THE GRAND FINALE VIA THE CLIMAX

HERE WE ARE; THE HOME STRETCH.

At the climax, your protagonist confronts his antagonist, resolving the central story conflict.

Maybe your protagonist thwarts the villain, kills the alien king, arrests the murderer, tells off his boss, defeats his rival, or rejects the wrong romantic prospect (and pursues the right one).

Regardless of what this one-on-one confrontation looks like, from the very beginning, you knew your story was headed in this direction. In contrast to the middle, you had a sense of what might go down.

Writing it should be easy.

Here's the thing: you're probably exhausted from dealing with the complexities of Act Two; in particular, making sure that it doesn't sag. At this point, you may have little energy leftover to allocate toward the climax.

When it comes time to draft a rough version of it, you're liable to give the climax short shrift. I see this happen all too often.

And it does not bode well for your story.

Let me explain. The climax, along with the resolution (which we will address in due course), is audiences' last experience with your screenplay or novel.

Their memories of it stand out.

A lot.

Consequently, these memories color audiences' perception of your *entire* story.

In essence, audience delight over a dazzling middle can become buried underneath their disappointment with a mediocre ending. Thus, audiences are unlikely to enthusiastically recommend your story to their friends or colleagues.

How can they, when you haven't followed through?

Consider yourself forewarned: the climax isn't the time to be perfunctory. It's the time to go all out, to bring on the pomp.

Make sure your story climax feels momentous. Grace it with

a sense of occasion. To achieve this, try implementing one (or more) of the following three tactics:

(1) Select a spectacular setting.

Landmarks are an excellent choice as a backdrop for your climax. Their inherent significance will automatically imbue your climax with a sense of momentousness.

Think of Thornhill's attempt to save Eve in *North by Northwest*. The backdrop of Mount Rushmore makes the sequence a hundred times more memorable that it would be otherwise, minus the landmark.

Of course, you don't have to rely on a preexisting setting. You can build one from scratch.

If you opt for this route, remember that *you* control the layout. Take advantage of this freedom. Design a setting that's conducive to the kind of jaw-dropping stunts that will thrill your readers.

If there isn't a waterfall or a helipad or a twisty mountain road—and you'd like one—then put it in!

(2) Amplify the urgency.

Give your protagonist only minutes or seconds to achieve an objective or reach a destination. This device is commonly referred to as a *ticking clock*.

The clock may tick down while the protagonist is trying to accomplish his main goal; while he, having achieved his main goal, tries to return home; or both. By the way, despite its name, it doesn't have to be depicted with a physical clock.

By determining where your protagonist is racing through and racing toward, notice that the setting takes care of itself. Depending on the genre of your story, the urgency may be enough to compensate for a setting that's only so-so.

In *The Hangover*, for instance, once Phil, Alan, and Stu have found Doug, they must beat the clock and deliver Doug to his wedding on time. The settings involved (the interstate, the wedding venue) aren't terribly interesting. However, the urgency of the protagonists' situation gives the sequence a dash of zing.

If you're writing a romance or a romantic comedy, you've probably been advised not to end your story with a race to the airport. Without major tweaking, it's too cliché.

This is sound advice—but it's not the race that's the problem. It's the airport destination that makes the sequence feel trite. Keep this in mind when designing your ticking clock.

(3) Showcase a crucial choice your protagonist must make.

Perhaps your climax will feel momentous because it revolves around a critical choice, one that your entire story (or, at least, a fair proportion of it) has been building toward.

A textbook example can be found in *The Devil Wears Prada*. As the film progresses, Andy transforms into one of the fashion-obsessed girls she once scoffed at. She can remain in this world, ultimately becoming as demanding and calculating as her boss—or she can leave it. At the end of the climax, Andy chooses to leave.

In *Lord of the Rings: The Fellowship of the Ring*, two crucial choices are made at the climax: reneging on his vow, Boromir tries to seize the One Ring from Frodo. As a result of Boromir's betrayal, Frodo decides to cast off the protection of the Fellowship and embark on his journey alone.

The summit of Amon Hen, the setting of *The Fellowship*'s climax, is not as spectacular as Helm's Deep or Minas Tirith (and its environs), the climactic settings of the second and third films, respectively, in the trilogy. Yet, *The Fellowship*'s climax holds its own, even though the scale of the action is limited by its comparatively mundane setting. This is due, in part, to the emotional impact of both Boromir's and Frodo's choices.

To be sure, there's more to crafting a climax that makes the grade. (And in my writing guide, *Story Climax*, I cover what to do in detail.) But for now, just by implementing one (or more) of these three tactics—setting, urgency, and choice—you have a reasonable degree of assurance that your climax won't drastically fall short of the mark.

Trough-Climax Compatibility

Usually, your protagonist's climactic plan will emerge from the circumstances of his trough. In other words (assuming a happy ending), his victory will be built on the ashes of failure.

Hence, it's a sound strategy to evaluate the compatibility of these two plot points. At this stage, you might not be able to see how to take your protagonist from his Act Two defeat to the Act Three climax.

The bridge is vague.

Unclear.

Invisible.

That's okay. You'll find a way when you outline. You may have to make minor (or major) modifications, but you'll find a way. Trust the process.

At the same time, it's possible that a trough type you may've previously set aside will work better with what you have now. Accordingly, you should review troughs from your discard pile in light of how you plan to develop the climax.

When you start pairing them up, a new trough-climax combination may leap out, jumpstarting your imagination. You'll get those tingles that indicate that you're on to something, something good.

If that's the case, run with it. Completely discard the trough type you initially chose, or even better, find a way to combine your old selection with your new choice.

ACTION STEP(S)

(19a) Briefly describe the climax of your story.

In a few sentences, describe some of the actions your protagonist must take as he confronts his antagonist during their final showdown.

(19b) Incorporate an element of momentousness into the climax.

If not present already, "bring out the pomp" during your story climax. Use one (or more) of the three tactics discussed in this chapter.

Because writers tend to wimp out here—and because the effect of this tendency is so damaging—I'm going to insist on greater specificity than I usually do:

FOR SETTING: Draw a map or architectural sketch of the location you've chosen (or are designing) to be the backdrop of your climax. For inspiration, look at travel-themed reference guides or pin boards on Pinterest.

FOR URGENCY: Describe the environment your protagonist is racing through and toward. Be specific. During his race, what are other characters (the antagonist, a sidekick, the stakes, etc.) doing?

Now, combine these actions into a short list, making sure to intercut between each character. Does this constellation of events make you feel tense? If not, it's back to the drawing board.

FOR CHOICE: Clearly articulate what your protagonist must choose between. How long has he been grappling with this choice? (You can be less specific here; e.g. since the midpoint.) Finally, in a few sentences, explain why this choice will feel significant to audiences.

(20) Analyze the climax's compatibility with the trough.

Examine the trough(s) you've selected in action steps #18a–c along with the climax you've described in steps #19a–b.

Replace your previously chosen trough type(s) (or, perhaps, modify your climax) if the changes will yield a more exciting story. Avoid changes that make your story easier to write—but less exciting to read.

- chapter fourteen -

TYING UP LOOSE ENDS VIA THE RESOLUTION

In comparison to most of the other major plot points, the resolution will, proportionally, take up very little of your story.

Nevertheless, for the same reason as the climax (it's part of audiences' last experience with your screenplay or novel), the resolution should not be tacked on to your story like an afterthought.

It requires due consideration—more so than its length might indicate.

From chapter 8, you already know that resolutions generally come in three forms, which are based on the outcome of the climax:

- happy (the protagonist achieves his goal)

- tragic (the protagonist fails to achieve his goal)
- bittersweet (the protagonist achieves his goal, but at great cost)

Thus, once the climax ends, you must depict its aftermath in a satisfying way. Typically, this entails showing how your protagonist (or his circumstances) has—as a consequence of his ordeals—changed.

To create your *hallmark of change* (or hallmarks; there can be more than one!), an easy and effective method is to take an element from your story's beginning and "turn it on its head" as part of your story's ending.

As an alternative, you can work backward: take your happy, tragic, or bittersweet ending; modify an element of it; and incorporate this modification into your story's beginning.

Neither approach is better than the other; it all depends on which component (the beginning or ending) you see more clearly.

When you have a solid grasp of your story's theme, oftentimes, you'll have a clear picture of your ending. You'll be able to visualize it in your mind's eye. In this case, working backward should be your best bet.

If you don't know your story's theme, don't fret. It may not have one. If it does have one (you just don't know what it is, specifically), again, don't worry. Possibilities will become evident when you comb through your outline and look for common threads. Instead of working backward to designate your hallmark of change, start with your story's beginning (which you should have some sense of, after completing action step #16).

To convey your hallmark of change, your protagonist doesn't have to return to his everyday world from your story's beginning. Although many resolutions unfold like this (especially in comedies), it's not a requirement.

How Long Does Your Resolution Have to Be?

We already touched on this topic. Resolutions don't have to be lengthy; they can be brief. It's a matter of how much space you need to do what needs to be done.

In order for audiences to experience the full effect of your hallmark of change, you may have to build up toward it. For it to make sense, you may need to take time to set the stage. It all depends on your story.

Look at *Rocky*. The resolution is brief, lasting little over a minute, and yet, the hallmarks of change are quite clear. Rocky has just gone fifteen rounds with the world heavyweight champion—a far contrast to Rocky's three-rounder with Spider where we first met the titular underdog. Plus, Rocky has secured Adrian's love—again, a far cry from the beginning when she could barely mumble three words to him.

You can see a similar pattern in *Seabiscuit*, when Seabiscuit wins the Santa Anita Handicap. Atypically, Seabiscuit's victory in the race isn't shown, but implied. But, like *Rocky*'s, the brief resolution achieves everything it has to do.

The victory creates an instant hallmark of change, contrasting with a previous failure to win the handicap (not from the story's beginning, but still effective) when Red's error caused Seabiscuit to lose the race. The contrast is further enhanced by Red's voiceover narration, which emphasizes how Seabiscuit's spirit has affected the three protagonists, restoring them from their previous state of brokenness.

When taking stock of the length of your resolution, also take accounting into account!

By the end of your screenplay or novel, you must tie up loose ends: answer unanswered questions and resolve unresolved conflicts. In addition, in a mystery, double-check that you've satisfactorily addressed all your red herrings. Traditionally, the resolution is the go-to location to take care of all of this. All the same, there is a limit. You can't go overboard and stuff *all* your explanations into the resolution.

Again, since this is audiences' last experience with your story, don't settle for a dry exchange to tidy up loose ends.

Dress up your explanation.

Make it good, make it interesting.

By the end of *Sherlock Holmes* (2009), Holmes has successfully thwarted Lord Blackwood. Still, one mystery remains. At the film's beginning, Blackwood was hanged. Watson even pronounced him dead. Hence, the film must explain how Blackwood managed to fake his own death.

Here's what the not-so-interesting version of the scene would look like: Watson asks Holmes how it was done, and Holmes answers with characteristic arrogance. As a matter of fact, a version like this occurs in one screenplay draft (dated March 2008, and written by Mike Johnson, with revisions by Anthony

Peckham)—only Lestrade, not Watson, poses the question to Holmes.

Happily for audiences, the film goes for more than a simple Q&A session. Watson walks into Holmes's apartment, while Holmes—in an attempt to re-create the scene—hangs from the ceiling. From this unusual position, Holmes explains how Blackwood escaped from the hangman's noose.

The parlor tricks don't stop there. When Watson eventually cuts Holmes down from the ceiling beam, Holmes describes the toxin Blackwood used to trick Watson into rendering an incorrect medical diagnosis.

But again, this information isn't conveyed only through dialogue. To reach his deduction, Holmes has experimented on Watson's dog—who lies, paralyzed, with paws outstretched, on the floor. (Don't worry animal lovers! He recovers without any apparent side effects.)

These changes are minor really, not terribly elaborate. Yet, their payoff is handsome. Compared to the standard Q&A, this scene is more dramatic. More memorable. Funnier too.

A model worth emulating.

In sum, when you're tying up loose ends at the end of your story, don't be perfunctory about it.

Your obligation to entertain audiences doesn't stop once your protagonist, as a result of the climax, stops pursuing his goal.

Your obligation continues until the last page.

• • •

At this point, you know quite a bit about your story's structural code. To quickly recap, you know the:

- opening image (your point of entry)
- inciting incident
- first-act break
- midpoint
- trough
- climax
- resolution (well, you'll know this once you complete the action steps at the end of this chapter, *smile*)

An impressive amount—and gleaned in a super-short period of time too!

However, you'll notice that two essential plot points are missing from this list: the fork and the closing image.

These plot points are important. The fork is a good indicator that your characters are facing the kind of dilemmas that keep audiences riveted; while the closing image, among other things, helps reinforce your theme.

But you can take care of them later. You don't need to know them in advance to fill in the remaining plot points in your outline—the topic we'll tackle in the next four chapters.

Before we get to that, a quick note. We've covered the basics of story structure, enough to help you generate an outline and construct a solid foundation for your story. But there's more to story structure—it's a big topic!

If you're interested in taking your knowledge further, and want to learn how to use story structure to avoid the kind of problems that audiences often gripe about, check out my writing guides on the inciting incident, midpoint, trough, and climax. Learn more by visiting this link:

➡ http://scribemeetsworld.com/books/#structure

Or, if you learn better with visuals and video (or want a faster route to structure mastery), consider enrolling in my online course, Smarter Story Structure. For more details, type this link into your web browser:

➡ http://scribemeetsworld.com/3AS/

Okay, quick side note over. Complete the action steps below, then continue on to Part III, where you'll learn how to finish the rest of your outline using a method backed by scientific research!

ACTION STEP(S)

(21a) Determine your story's resolution.

Is it happy? Tragic? Or bittersweet?

If bittersweet, describe the cost your protagonist must pay to achieve victory.

(21b) Designate a hallmark of change.

If you can't clearly picture the ending of your story, revisit your notes on your story opening from action step #16. Select an element from your notes, modify this element, and then build your resolution around it.

If you can clearly picture the ending of your story, select an element from your visualization, modify this element, and then incorporate it into your notes from action step #16.

(22) Get a jumpstart on your accounting.

Based on what you currently know, jot down everything that needs to be accounted for by the end of your screenplay or novel.

If you only know a few specifics about your story, the only thing you may write down on your paper is the heading, *Things That Need to Be Accounted For by the End of My Screenplay or Novel*. You'll just add to this paper as you go along.

Totally cool. Like action step #18c, this step is designed to help you cultivate a helpful habit; in this case, keeping tabs on all your loose ends.

As an alternative, you may find it more convenient to (1) mark loose ends (in brackets, perhaps) on your finished outline or rough draft; (2) transfer these notes onto a separate sheet of paper; and (3) use this paper as a checklist during editing.

NOTES FOR PART II

Chapter 9

6. J. J. Abrams, "The Mystery Box" (TED Talk, March 2007), http://www.ted.com/talks/j_j_abrams_mystery_box.

- PART III -

HOW TO OUTLINE YOUR STORY WITH A METHOD BACKED BY SCIENTIFIC RESEARCH (SORT OF), A.K.A. EXCAVATING STORY FOSSILS

IN THEORY, HAVING CRACKED THE STRUCTURAL CODE OF YOUR STORY, you could start a rough draft right now, this very instant.

You have a framework to support your story idea, enabling you to showcase your concept to best effect. You have several bearings to write toward, enabling you to face the blank page without panicking.

Despite these dual benefits, I encourage you not to rush into your rough draft just yet. Instead, take time to fill in the blanks, i.e. the in-betweens, the intervening plot points between each structural signpost.

Here's why: there's a difference between *what* and *how*.

What do I mean by that?

If you don't figure out the in-betweens beforehand, you'll have to figure them out as you go along. Sure, with your story structure already in place, this shouldn't be terribly daunting. But it does place an additional burden on your imagination, muse, creative faculty—whatever you like to call the magical force that spins story from thin air. You must figure out not only what happens next…but also how each event unfolds.

In contrast, when you've already figured out the in-betweens, you already know what happens next. Thus, you can devote *all* your energy to figuring out how to make those plot points as interesting, engaging, and unique as possible.

This, by the way, is why you shouldn't worry that outlining will produce a "paint by the numbers" kind of story. With so much energy devoted toward expressing your plot points in new, imaginative ways, the final result should be anything but predictable.

That's not to say that you can't do both at the same time. Figure out the what and the how simultaneously. However, it stands to reason that dealing with one at a time is the infinitely easier (and less stressful) option.

Plus, it's more efficient. You need a full list of plot points in hand in order to identify most of your story's plot holes and problem spots. Once you've identified them, you can fix them. Since you're working with an outline, inserting fixes requires tweaking a few words or sentences—which takes a lot less time than rewriting hundreds (even thousands) of words in a rough draft.

As a quick reminder, how to identify (and fix) problem spots in an outline so you can produce a cleaner rough draft, is beyond the scope of this book. I'm just pointing out it's another benefit of figuring out the in-betweens—the focus of this writing guide. (By the way, if you're interested in writing cleaner rough drafts, check out the third book in the Iterative Outlining series, *Sparkling Story Drafts*.)

If I conducted a quick poll right now, we'd be in agreement, right? It is worth your time to figure out the in-betweens. Now the question remains, how to do it?

Answering this question requires another metaphor (are you surprised?), but before we switch up analogies, I have to backtrack...

...to when I first tried my hand at writing a novel. Then, my inner critic was like a strict club bouncer. Words of all kinds were barred entry. He worked overtime too, applying his no-admittance policies not just when I was working on a rough draft, but also when I was outlining. Almost every idea I had was deemed unworthy.

Through trial and error, I found there were a few things that, somehow, forced my critic to take a break, enabling me to make headway. This is one of them: I told myself that I wasn't creating something new.

My outline—my story—both already existed.

I just had to uncover them.

This thought was enormously comforting. I no longer had to bear the burden of creation. Someone else had already taken care of it, had already done the hard work of fitting all the pieces together. *I* didn't have to painstakingly build something from scratch. No siree!

My job was far simpler. I just had to dredge up a preexisting work. That was all.

In my imagination, this preexisting work was composed of bones buried in the ground by their original creator. All I had to do was dig them up, brush them off, and assemble them correctly. Because the pressure was suddenly off of me, outlining my story (and, later on, writing my rough draft) became less daunting. Correspondingly, my inner critic became less of a taskmaster, and my index cards and computer pages filled up more speedily than they had before.

Years later, I discovered that Stephen King shares the same philosophy—that stories are preexisting things—right down to the bone analogy! In his book *On Writing*, this is how he eloquently describes it:

> Stories are found things, like fossils in the ground…Stories aren't souvenir tee-shirts or GameBoys. Stories are relics, part of an undiscovered preexisting world. The writer's job is to use the tools in his or her toolbox to get as much of each one out of the ground intact as possible. Sometimes the fossil you uncover is small; a seashell. Sometimes it's enormous, a *Tyrannosaurus Rex* with all those gigantic ribs and grinning teeth.

However, although Stephen King and I agree that stories are preexisting things, we diverge on a salient point: how to uncover them.

He's skeptical of plotting out a story in advance, whereas I'm an unabashed fan of it. That's what outlining is for me—drumroll, please! a new metaphor is on its way—it's merely digging up the bones of my preexisting story.

Over time, I developed a system to excavate these bones as efficiently as possible. First, when I begin my fossil hunt, I seek out specific bones—the ones belonging to my story's structure. In Part II, these were conceptualized as numbers belonging to a code, but in keeping with our new archeology analogy, we can reconceptualize them as the vertebrae, or spine, of a story.

Having excavated these bones, I use them to guide my search for the in-betweens, the fossils that remain. To hunt for these remaining fossils, I use something I've dubbed the *walkenwright method*. (The reason for its name—a play on *walk and write*—will shortly become apparent.)

In the following chapters, I'll describe this method in greater detail. I'll start with an overview of the walkenwright method—walk you through it, so to speak (sorry, couldn't resist the pun!).

Then I'll explain the rationale behind it (this is where the scientific research can be found) and show you five simple ways to make it more effective (number four is real fun).

Lastly, I'll run through a thorough set of frequently asked questions about the walkenwright method and provide you with nine outlining alternatives (just for kicks).

Admittedly, the walkenwright method is a bit radical, but if you embrace it, you will have a full list of your story's plot points in as little as 2 hours.

Exciting thought, isn't it?

Dust off your shovels. It's time to go digging!

- chapter fifteen -

AN OVERVIEW OF THE OUTLINING METHOD

As a quick sketch, this is how you outline your story using the walkenwright method: you go for a walk.

As you walk, you brainstorm (aloud or in your head; whichever feels more comfortable) possible ways to fill in the gaps between two plot points that you already defined during Part II of this writing guide. (For the sake of illustration, we'll call one of them Plot Point A, and the other Plot Point G.)

To return to our fossil analogy, while you're walking, you're collecting bones that potentially belong to your story.

Subplots, complications, set pieces that you didn't reflect on beforehand—all of these (and more) will suddenly materialize.

New characters (including, perhaps, additional antagonists) whom you didn't know existed will walk right into your scenes—almost as if mimicking your own movements.

Your story will open up in ways you didn't expect, detouring into thrilling directions that you had no inkling about when you first began your walkenwright session.

If you're a hardcore pantser who's tentatively begun to embrace outlining, bring out the forks because this is a have-your-cake-and-eat-it situation. See, *this* is where the joy of discovery takes place.

It's still there; it hasn't vanished.

It's just occurring at an earlier stage in the writing process, *before* your rough draft instead of *during* it. Such an arrangement enables you to increase your productivity, and yet, enjoy the satisfaction of spontaneous creation.

When you're brainstorming ideas during your walk, you probably won't have to prompt your imagination much. Just by giving it starting (Plot Point A) and end (Plot Point G) targets, it should easily fill in the missing details.

But if your imagination needs a nudge, remind it about your logline and the genre of your story. Reflecting on these two elements, after repeating to yourself what you've come up with so far, should get it going again.

If not, you can also ask yourself questions, like:

- What step could my protagonist take that would bring him closer to Plot Point G?

- When my protagonist tries to take this step, what kind of setback could occur?
- What would my protagonist do in response? Would he seek out help? From whom? What would this potential helper suggest?
- Having encountered a setback, complication, or surprising development, what is my protagonist's new plan?
- What is the antagonist doing while my protagonist is taking steps toward his goal? What are other characters doing?
- What kind of fun stuff do audiences expect to find in my genre? How can I bring these elements into the plot?
- What could happen next? (An obvious question, to be sure, but nevertheless, very effective as a prompt. Don't underestimate it!)

Your answers will encompass a broad range of specificity. Sometimes, a clear picture of what's happening will flash in your mind's eye. Other times, you'll only know the gist of the plot point. Everything else is very vague.

In a romance, for example, you may come up with a plot point that's as general as "the hero and heroine go on a date that ends badly, and she doesn't want to see him again."

Alternatively, it may be more specific: "The hero takes the heroine to a carnival, and wins her a stuffed animal (a pink turtle). But the heroine's ex-husband is there too, and he tosses the toy into the mud. Embarrassed by the scene, the heroine decides to break it off with the hero."

In a heist film, a plot point may be as simple as "something happens with the getaway cars." Or, it could be more complex: "When the protagonist tries to steal cars from the impound lot, he's caught by a corrupt cop, who blackmails the protagonist into stealing vital evidence—destined for a high-profile courtroom trial—while it's in transit."

Either will do; whether specific or vague, you have something to work with. That's what matters.

Don't concern yourself overly much with how your plot points unfold. If you know, great! If you don't, no biggie. There'll be time enough for that later, during stage 3 of iterative outlining.

How much is enough?

That is, how many plot points between Plot Point A and Plot Point G do you need to have before moving on to the next step of the walkenwright method? (Remember, G was an arbitrary letter, chosen for the sake of illustration.)

I'd aim for 8–12, but this is just a rough estimate. The ideal number depends on format (screenplay, novel, novella, serial, etc.) and genre (a category romance novel will require far fewer total plot points than an epic fantasy; a comedy script is usually 10–20 pages shorter than a drama).

At this point, I'm guessing that this process seems fairly cut and dried. You're walking and brainstorming. Standard stuff for a writer, and even when united together, the combination is hardly revolutionary at all.

Here's where the radical part comes in: you're walking, and you're brainstorming…*but you're not writing anything down.*

And you're not going to. Not yet.

After generating a list of story events from Plot Point A to Plot Point G (we'll call this micro-iteration #1), don't pause. Keep on walking. Repeat the process, generating micro-iteration #2, i.e. another set of story events from Plot Point A to Plot Point G.

On your second micro-iteration, you'll discover that new characters and events, which didn't appear during micro-iteration #1, may walk into your story now, while some that were present before will be thrown "overboard." Events will shuffle around too—maybe a little, maybe a lot.

Continue to repeat the process, going through micro-iterations #3, #4, #5, etc., until a consistent chronology, featuring the same players and the same events, emerges. When you can repeat *this* set of plot points three times to yourself (slight variance is okay)—that's when you write everything down. This is what I call your *keeper micro-iteration.*

To facilitate recording, carry a pen and a notebook with you. If that's cumbersome, then stash your writing materials (pen and paper, laptop, etc.) in your car, and choose a place to walk that isn't too far from where you've parked.

When you're scribbling down the list of plot points from your keeper micro-iteration (let's say it was your fifth micro-iteration), a few things might happen: (1) something from a previous micro-iteration that you've long since dropped may make a reappearance, (2) you think of alternatives to the plot points you've settled on as part of your keeper micro-iteration, and (3) you get ideas for plot points beyond the range of your current walkenwright session (e.g. those that occur between Plot Points H and M).

If such tangential ideas come to you—no matter how amazing they are—ignore them. At least temporarily. First focus on penning to paper the list of plot points from your keeper micro-iteration (in this example, #5); these are your top priority. After that, you can explore tangential ideas to your heart's content.

That's it for your first walkenwright session. Follow the same procedure for the rest of your walkenwright sessions (there'll be four total; refer to the action steps at the end of chapter 18 for more details)—with one important caveat.

For each subsequent session, to get back into your brainstorming groove, it's a good idea to review the last 4–5 plot points from the previous session's keeper micro-iteration. (That's the recommended minimum. Ideally, you'll review all of its plot points, not just the last four or five.) *But rely on your memory alone.* Don't consult your notes from the previous day. I'll explain why later on, in chapter 17. For the time being, just take my word for it.

When you mentally rehearse plot points from a previous walkenwright session (from Day 1, let's say), you may come up with a variation that you like even better than what you actually recorded on Day 1.

If so, brainstorm ideas for Day 2 (i.e. your current walkenwright session) in light of this new variation, and make a note of the change when you finally record Day 2's keeper micro-iteration… but don't go back to your notes from Day 1.

Again, your priority is to make today's keeper micro-iteration the best it can be, not to improve the micro-iteration from a previous session.

Of course, your final product should be one cohesive whole. Eventually, you'll have to assess what kind of ripple effect this new variation will cause, and how it may alter the plot points you wrote down on Day 1. But you can take care of that later.

Speaking of time, each walkenwright session shouldn't take you long. The total time you spend depends on a variety of factors, mainly:

- how familiar you are with your genre
- how comfortable you become with the walkenwright method
- how much of your story you've already uncovered by completing the action steps from Parts I and II of this book
- how fast you write down your keeper micro-iteration

On average, each walkenwright session should take about 20–25 minutes.

Four walkenwright sessions, 20–25 minutes each.

You know what that means, right?

You'll have an outline for your entire story in less than 2 hours.

Yes, less than 2 hours!

Pretty incredible, no?

By making this modest investment of time up front, you'll always know what happens next in your screenplay or novel—maximizing your confidence as you dash out your rough draft, and ultimately, minimizing the time it'll take you to revise it.

- chapter sixteen -

THE RATIONALE BEHIND THE METHOD (THE SCIENCE STUFF IS HERE)

THE RATIONALE BEHIND THE WALKING ASPECT OF the walkenwright method is easy to understand.

Indeed, you might already be familiar with it. When you've faced a thorny plot issue, you yourself have probably taken a walk to help you clear your head and find a solution.

You're in good company.

Beethoven would take "a vigorous walk after lunch…to record chance musical thoughts." [7] Steve Jobs, too, was a fan of walking, as Walter Isaacson's biography reveals. "It was his preferred way to have a serious conversation." [8]

To bring it back to writers, in *On Writing*, Stephen King mentions that he cultivated a habit of walking when he suffered from writer's block while working on *The Stand*. "I spent those walks being bored and thinking about my gigantic boondoggle of a manuscript."

My feeling is this: why limit its scope?

Why should writers use walking only as an analytical tool?

Why not broaden its application, and use walking to generate a story plot in its entirety, rather than just to solve plot holes?

As a matter of fact, walking appears to boost brain power (certainly a handy benefit!). As Ferris Jabr summarizes in the *New Yorker*:

> **Walking on a regular basis also promotes new connections between brain cells, staves off the usual withering of brain tissue that comes with age, [and] increases the volume of the hippocampus (a brain region crucial for memory). [9]**

Wait. It gets better.

Walking doesn't just bestow you with advantages that are wonderful to have in life, in general. Walking can also benefit writers—all creatives—in particular. That's because research conducted at Stanford by Marily Oppezzo and Daniel Schwartz indicates that walking facilitates creative thinking. [10]

In one experiment conducted by the Stanford researchers, participants had to come up with alternative uses for various items, a test that measures divergent thinking and "depends on cognitive flexibility." As an example, an alternative use for a button would be "a tiny strainer."

Responses were considered creative if they were both appropriate and novel. Novelty was determined by rules reminiscent of the game Scattergories. That is, if two people came up with the idea of using a button as a strainer, their response—although appropriate—wouldn't count because it wouldn't be "unique within the sample of participants."

Oppezzo and Schwartz found that participants who walked while generating ideas for alternative uses performed better than participants who were sedentary, *with a 60% average increase in creative output.*

That's not all. In another experiment, the researchers used a different kind of creativity-measuring test, in which participants, when prompted, produced analogies instead of alternative uses. A prompt might be something like "a candle burning low." Participants were asked to take the core idea behind the prompt, in this case "a positive force extinguishing itself" and transpose it into a new environment, e.g. "the last hand of a gambler's last game." Intriguingly, according to Oppezzo and Schwartz (citing Eysenck's *Genius; The natural history of creativity*), when compared to other professionals, famous writers excel at this test.

Again, participants who walked while generating their answers performed better than those who did not. "100% of those who walked outside generated at least one novel high-quality analogy compared with 50% of those seated inside."

100% vs. 50%. Big difference!

Without going into detail, high-quality answers had to fulfill specific criteria (in case you were wondering). To the prompt of "a budding cocoon," two high-quality analogies would be "coming out of a meditation retreat" and "an apprentice coming out of the shadows of his master." (As an aside, I think the apprentice response is pretty darn clever, don't you?)

What's really fascinating is how the participants teased out their analogical answers. It mirrors the iterative nature of the walkenwright method. As the researchers described it, "People talked through the base prompts, *iterating* to find the deep structure of the prompt" [emphasis mine].

Although Oppezzo and Schwartz have demonstrated that walking facilitates creativity, the mechanics behind the phenomenon are still up for debate. In an interview with the *New York Times*, Oppezzo conjectured that walking could create a positive mental state where creativity can blossom, or as an alternative possibility, "walking may divert energy that otherwise would be devoted, intentionally or not, to damping down wild, creative thought." [11]

Regardless of the reason, the connection is clear. Walking spurs on creativity. Whether you wholeheartedly embrace the walkenwright method or not, it's a smart move to incorporate walks into your writing process.

Okay, I'm Convinced About the Importance of Walking...But Why Can't I Write Anything Down?

According to Mason Currey, author of *Daily Rituals*, famous composers such as Tchaikovsky, Mahler, and Beethoven would all take daily strolls to jumpstart their creativity. However, in contrast to the walkenwright model, they paused to record their ideas as they went along. [12]

Sensible behavior, certainly.

At first glance, it may seem absurd not to follow their lead—downright crazy to plot out a quarter of your story without a safety net in place. And right now, you may be balking at the suggestion.

Despite appearances, there is a good reason for doing it this way. To my knowledge, it's not backed by scientific research. It comes from personal observation and experience. Here it is: if you immediately write down micro-iteration #1 of your story, it's easy to settle for the "low-hanging fruit." (Yes, I'm tossing yet another metaphor into the mix!)

Once you commit your list of plot points to paper, you might not have the wherewithal to dig deeper: to discard ideas that are irrelevant, incompatible, illogical, or inferior. Satisfied that you made progress with your outline, you'll happily move on to another, less taxing, activity.

Of course, with time, you can mold this material into better shape, into something that more closely approximates the final version of your story. But we're trying to shortcut the process (as much as is possible) here. That's what the walkenwright method does.

It forces you to reach higher *now*.

Because you're walking and not writing down your ideas, you don't have the time to become attached to the ones you're better off rejecting. Free from this attachment, your imagination can quickly and easily discard the weaker material and improve what remains with each micro-iteration—increasing the odds that everything you generate is, to extend our fruit metaphor, of "export quality."

In point of practice, this won't be the case. Even though each micro-iteration should incrementally improve your story, the final one you write down at the end of each walkenwright session, i.e. your keeper micro-iteration, will inevitably require modification.

Sometimes, a lot; sometimes, a little. It varies.

Still, because you've already made improvements on the fly, as you were walking, you should have less pruning to do. You'll be in a stronger, more advantageous position.

To sum it up, it should take you significantly less time to produce more raw material of decent quality than it would have, had you paused to commit each iteration to paper.

- chapter seventeen -

5 SIMPLE THINGS YOU CAN DO TO SECURE THE COOPERATION OF YOUR CREATIVE GENIUS

LET'S TALK ABOUT THE SUBCONSCIOUS MIND FOR a minute.

It absorbs and processes everything you experience—whether consciously or subliminally. Your imagination pulls from this subconscious pool to produce the raw material for your story.

As summarized in the previous chapter, with the walkenwright method, your imagination should produce a high proportion of usable material within a short span of time. Yet, as with any method, there are ways to maximize its effectiveness.

For best results, when conducting your walkenwright sessions, you should try to secure the full cooperation of your subconscious mind and your imagination (which, together, form what I like to call your *creative genius*).

Below are five simple ways to accomplish this:

(1) Scout for the ideal location.

Choose a place where you can walk "on autopilot," for at least an eighth of a mile at a time. Any shorter, and you may feel like you're pacing rather than walking.

You don't want your creative energies to be distracted by the fear of collision—which means that your normal walking hangouts might not be suitable for this purpose.

Walking around your neighborhood will work, but only if you don't have to cross the street every few minutes to reach the next section of sidewalk.

Speaking of sidewalks, choose ones that are even. Once you hit your groove, you'll probably be too engrossed in your task to take heed of bumpy, uneven spots in the sidewalk. (Uneven terrain is one reason why hiking trails get a black mark, even though they're peaceful and scenic.)

Parks and beaches can also be conducive, but steer clear of them during peak hours, when collisions with dogs, volleyballs, etc. are more likely to occur. If you live in a place like California, where parks and beaches tend to be quite vast, you may wander far away from your car (where your writing materials are likely stashed).

To minimize the delay between the time you finalize each session's plot points and the time you write them down, carry your writing tools with you. Alternatively, construct your walking routine so that you cycle between or around places that are not too far away from your car. In other words, don't venture too deep into the park or the beach!

Actually, walking in a loop (rather than on an extended path) can carry an extra advantage. Because you're simultaneously cycling through multiple micro-iterations of your story, your outward movements will match the circular pattern of your inner thoughts. The synchronicity could facilitate the brainstorming process.

My vote for the ideal location?

An outdoor high school or college track that's open to the public. You get a premade loop with little potential for collision.

(2) Grab comfortable gear.

Wear comfortable clothing and shoes. Nothing too small or too tight.

100% cotton. Stretchy waistbands. Broken-in sneakers.

These are your friends.

Again, you want your mind to focus on your story. You don't want it to be distracted by pain in your pinkie toe or by the concern that your jeans are giving you a "muffin top."

(3) Embrace optimism.

Before each walkenwright session, rub your hands together and tell yourself, "This is gonna be good."

It sounds cheesy, I know. And you may feel silly and awkward doing it. But it costs virtually nothing (just a nick to your pride), and it can secure everything—a cooperative creative genius.

So why not?

(4) Get more sleep.

Scientific research suggests that sleeping, much like walking, facilitates creativity.

As Leslie Berlin summarizes in the *New York Times*, "Sleep assists the brain in flagging unrelated ideas and memories, forging connections among them that increase the odds that a creative idea or insight will surface." [13]

Want more specific research? No problem. In a study conducted at Lancaster University, participants had to solve word puzzles (known as RATs) that require creativity to answer. The researchers found that a bout of sleep enhanced the participants' ability to solve puzzles rated as difficult. Interestingly, sleep didn't confer an advantage for puzzles that were rated as being easy. [14]

Oh, I've got more. Actually, I've got an impressive statistic: research conducted at Harvard by Dr. Ellenbogen "indicates that if an incubation period includes sleep, people are 33% more likely to infer connections among distantly related ideas." [15] (Remember, making such connections is at the heart of being creative.)

Hold on a second. Don't rush to put on your jammies just yet.

Sleep isn't as simple as it may seem. The studies described above examined sleep…well, as sleep. But it's not homogenous.

In fact, it comes in two forms: REM (rapid eye movement) sleep and NREM (non–rapid eye movement) sleep. They alternate within a period that lasts about 90 minutes, and a night's slumber will typically include 4–5 of these 90-minute cycles. During REM sleep, you dream. During NREM, your body repairs itself.

Now, as far as I can tell, the studies listed above (by Lancaster University and by Dr. Ellenbogen) didn't discriminate between REM and NREM sleep. This doesn't invalidate their results. All the same, if we want to know whether one form of sleep yields a greater creative advantage than the other, we have to look elsewhere.

Anecdotal evidence suggests that REM sleep facilitates creativity more than NREM sleep. The periodic table of elements [16], the riff to "(I Can't Get No) Satisfaction" by the Rolling Stones [17], and the premise behind the blockbuster Twilight franchise [18]—all came to their creators via a dream.

Experiments conducted at UC San Diego (UCSD) lend scientific credence to these anecdotes. In one experiment, participants took RATs (remember those? they're word puzzles that require creativity to solve) in the morning and afternoon. Between sessions, participants took a brief nap or listened to instrumental music.

If the participants had prior exposure to elements of the afternoon puzzles, and if they had managed to score some REM sleep during their nap, they displayed a 40% improvement over their baseline morning performance. [19]

No REM sleep, no improvement.

Putting this all together, while you're conducting your walkenwright sessions, your creativity will probably be at higher levels if you get a good night's sleep in general, and a decent amount of REM sleep in particular.

Recall that I recommended *not* to consult your notes when you're reviewing plot points from your previous day's walkenwright session. This is why.

In between the two sessions, you've "slept on it." During your slumber, your creative genius will still be interacting with the material you generated during the day—even though you're not consciously guiding it.

It may come up with fresh insight into how to connect the plot points of your story.

If you consult your notes, you'll be suppressing this insight.

On the other hand, if you ignore your notes and go by memory alone, this insight can bubble up and rise to the surface of your consciousness. Then, if you like, you can build your current walkenwright session's plot points on it.

In the UCSD experiment, REM sleep *and* priming were both necessary to improve participants' performance. Extrapolating these results onto storytelling, when you're about to fall asleep, try to prime your mind by mulling on the plot points you generated during the day as well as the plot point (like the midpoint) you'll be brainstorming toward on the following day.

Use a light touch. Don't forcefully seek connections. If you stress yourself out, it won't be easy for you to fall asleep, and you'll just undermine your efforts to enhance your creativity.

Speaking of, maximizing your sleep (both NREM and REM) is a topic worthy of its own book, but here are a few quickie tips to get you started:

ABSTAIN FROM DRINKING ALCOHOL. Why? Alcohol adversely affects REM sleep.

INVEST IN AN EYE MASK. Nighttime exposure to light can tamper with your body's production of melatonin, a hormone that helps you stay asleep (among other benefits).

SLEEP LONGER. As the night progresses, your proportion of REM sleep increases. If you only sleep for a few hours, you're not giving your body long enough to hit the high-density REM areas of the sleep cycle.

RESERVE YOUR BED FOR SLEEPING ONLY. Don't read (novels, work-related documents, lifestyle magazines, etc.) or watch TV in it. You shouldn't be reading novels or watching TV anyway (see tip #5, on conducting a genre fast), but in case you ignore tip #5, don't indulge in these activities in bed.

DON'T STAY IN BED IF YOU CAN'T FALL ASLEEP. If you're lying in bed for 15 minutes or so, and you haven't fallen asleep, get out of bed. Temporarily relocate to another (quiet) spot in your home. This way, your mind won't associate your bed with insomnia.

DON'T COUNT SHEEP. Instead of following this folk remedy for insomnia, picture a waterfall or a beach. Such relaxing scenes helped insomniacs to fall asleep 20 minutes sooner in a study conducted by Oxford researchers. Why is this approach better than sheep? According to Allison Harvey, "It's easier to stay with it because it's more interesting…counting sheep is just too mundane to effectively keep worries away." [20]

If interested, you can find additional sleep tips (including how to use the 4-7-8 breathing technique to alleviate anxiety) in an online article by Dr. Mercola. (For the link, see no. 21 in the notes section at the end of Part III.)

(5) At the very least, go on a genre fast.

It may surprise you to learn that bestselling crime novelist Michael Connelly reads "sparingly" when he writes. [22] As part of the walkenwright method, it's wise to follow Connelly's lead.

More specifically, I suggest that you steer clear of novels and films in the same genre as your work in progress (a) during your walkenwright sessions and (b) a few weeks prior to them.

Of course, you should familiarize yourself with the conventions in your genre and study the works of other writers who've mastered them. But this is not the time to do it. Why not? As Connelly succinctly explains, "It can be intrusive to your own work."

It's all too easy for your plot points to be pale imitations of the story you just enjoyed; all too easy for your creative genius to gravitate toward what you've recently read or watched.

Simply put, it's inconvenient not to.

Instead of taking the time to explore other, more "remote" options, your creative genius will proffer up derivative ideas based on what you've just experienced.

And it's all too easy for you to accept them—no questions asked.

To revisit our fossil-hunting analogy, instead of putting in the effort or time to dig up the bones belonging to *your* story, you'll be tempted to dip into another excavation site, steal a bone that's on prominent display, and use it to connect the pieces of your story together.

Although you might convince yourself otherwise, everyone will know that it's stolen property.

Note: This doesn't mean that when you brainstorm ideas for plot points, you can't use movies you've watched (or books you've read) as a frame of reference. That's fine. You just don't want your entire plot to be derivative, which is what the genre fast is intended to help you avoid.

What About Other Genres?

Reading books (or watching movies or TV shows) from genres other than your own certainly reduces the inclination to pull wholesale from someone else's work.

If you're writing a romance novel, you're unlikely to jam into it an element from the mystery you just read—at least not without the kind of tweaking that would make it feel original. As a bonus, such tweaks could add texture and nuance rarely found in your subgenre, helping your romance to stand out.

That said, even with other genres, you still need to be on your guard. Their effects can be subtle.

If you're reading a cynical non-fiction piece on banking fraud in

America, for example, your subconscious can temporarily absorb this author's pessimistic attitude. Consequently, this attitude can carry over into your own work.

Suddenly, your protagonist may engage in futile, fatalistic behaviors—not the direction you intended your story to take. Assuming you can pinpoint the problem later on (it's a tricky one to detect!), you'll have to waste time fixing it.

By extension, it's also a sound strategy to avoid activities that may cause you to temporarily absorb another person's voice. Things like: watching the nightly news, engaging in social media, or listening to podcasts.

Can I Do Anything Fun at All?

Sure.

But ideally, during your downtime, you'll engage in activities where the loudest voice in your head will be *yours*, not some other content creator's.

Possibilities include:

- soaking in the tub
- making a pizza crust or a three-tiered specialty cake from scratch
- organizing your bookshelves, desktop files, photo albums, kitchen cupboards, DVD collection, etc.
- going camping (if only in your own backyard)
- appreciating the sunset

- playing a musical instrument or a pickup game of basketball
- cross-stitching a pillow
- creating a collage of pictures that embody the characters, settings, and tone of your story

Remember, your abstention won't last long: the genre fast for a little over 3 weeks, the other types of fasting for about 10 days (4 days of walkenwriting, plus a buffer period the week prior). After you've completed your walkenwright sessions, you can, if you wish, reintroduce these activities back into your schedule.

- chapter eighteen -

FREQUENTLY ASKED QUESTIONS ABOUT THE METHOD

At this point, you have a broad overview of the walkenwright method and the rationale behind it, as well as specific tips on how to maximize its effectiveness.

Yet, some questions probably remain. In this chapter, I'll address the nitty-gritty details that weren't covered earlier on.

Without further ado, let's get down to it!

Do I have to walk? Can't I generate micro-iterations while sitting down?
No.

Walking is an essential component of the walkenwright method.

Under scouting locations, every place you mentioned was outdoors. Can I walk indoors?

As part of their study, Oppezzo and Schwartz examined whether walking outdoors facilitated creative thinking better than walking indoors. Although Oppezzo had predicted that "walking outside would blow everything out of the water," [23] "the effect of being outdoors was inconclusive" [24].

Even so, I suggest that walking outdoors should be your go-to option, and walking indoors should be a second choice (perhaps when the weather is poor, and it's not feasible to walk outside).

All too often, writers box their characters into static environments (bars and cars being two of the top offenders) that are not exciting to read about. I suspect that walking indoors would aggravate this inclination, but that is, admittedly, conjecture, so make of it what you will.

Do I have to conduct four walkenwright sessions?

At first, four sessions may seem daunting because (a) you're not used to this method, and (b) it means that you have to keep a quarter of your story in your head at a time.

If that's the case, break down each session into more manageable chunks. However, after a certain point, the more sessions you conduct, the more likely it is that the final product will lack cohesion. Unless your project is of epic length, I'd recommend a maximum of eight sessions.

On the off chance that you'd like to conduct fewer than four sessions, let me offer a word of caution. There's a limit to how many items your short-term memory can hold. Keeping in your head more than 15 (or so) plot points at a time is probably pushing it.

How should I schedule my walkenwright sessions?

When you're ready to develop a full outline of your story using the walkenwright method, make sure to pick a time in your schedule where you can devote four *consecutive* days to conduct your sessions.

If you're conducting more than four sessions (see the preceding FAQ), again, choose a time when you can conduct all of your sessions consecutively. For eight sessions, block out eight consecutive days.

You want to build up momentum over the course of each session. That's not going to happen if your sessions are scattered across a week…or more.

Plus, plot points from previous sessions should inform plot points from later sessions. The greater the interval between sessions, the more likely it is that you'll forget the direction you were heading toward (not to mention abandon your genre fast).

Correspondingly, the plot points you generate are less likely to add up to a cohesive whole. If you've abandoned your genre fast, your plot points may be derivative as well.

Also, limit yourself to one walkenwright session per day. This way, you'll enjoy a good night's sleep in between each session—and all the benefits that brings.

If you're pressed for time, I suppose you could cram two walkenwright sessions into one day—separating each with a nap that, ideally, is long enough to score you some REM sleep.

I'd avoid squeezing all your walkenwright sessions into one day unless your project is on the shorter side (e.g. a novella or serialized episode).

Why do I have to repeat my keeper micro-iteration three times before writing it down?

This way, you can be reasonably sure that what you've come up with isn't a fluke. You really have dug up the preexisting bones of your story.

I have trouble keeping track of my plot points before I write them down. Any tips?

This works for me. As you go along, tick off plot points on your fingers. For example:

Plot point #1: thumb, right hand

Plot point #2: index finger, right hand

Plot point #3: middle finger, right hand

Plot point #4: ring finger, right hand

Plot point #5: pinkie finger, right hand

Plot point #6: thumb, left hand

Plot point #7: index finger, left hand, etc.

For more than 10 plot points, I resume counting with my right hand. For example, I'd tick off plot point #11 with my right-hand thumb, plot point #12 with my right-hand index finger, etc.

I've found that this trick facilitates remembering the plot points when I cycle through my micro-iterations as well as when I write down my keeper micro-iteration. Let's say I'm having trouble remembering plot point #7. I ask myself, *What happened with the index finger of my left hand?*, stare at my finger for a bit, wiggle it around…and somehow, the memory comes back to me.

Additionally, here's a simple trick that seems too obvious to mention, but it really does make a difference. Number your notebook paper or computer document in advance, like so:

(1)

(2)

(3)

This way, you can write down your plot points (in proper order) immediately—decreasing the amount of time you have to hold them in your short-term memory (if only by a few seconds!).

Note: I've ended on #3 because this is simply an illustration. When you do it, you'll end on #12 (or, if you come up with more than 12 plot points, slightly beyond that).

I can't rely on my memory alone before I write down my plot points; I need more of a safety net. Can I say my micro-iterations aloud and record them with a microphone as I walk?
If this makes you feel more comfortable, then go for it. It shouldn't do any harm. That said, it may not be very beneficial either.

In most cases, you'll probably discover that reviewing the audio recording for each micro-iteration doesn't produce any nugget of value. And if it does, the nugget isn't worth the hassle.

If you can, try following this common prescription for heartache: if a woman wants to leave a relationship, the man should let her go (and vice versa). If their love is true, she'll return to him. If she doesn't, then they shouldn't have been a couple to begin with.

Likewise, if you come up with a spectacular plot point, but, somehow, forget it by the time you record your keeper micro-iteration, it will come back to you. At an opportune time too, not when it's too late to do anything about it. And if the idea doesn't come back to you…well then, it wasn't meant to be part of this story in the first place.

To be clear, this isn't a fail-safe. There is a possibility that, by not writing down your plot points until the end of your walkenwright session, you could lose something valuable. That hasn't been my personal experience, so I'm not worried about it.

But if you are, then by all means, record all your micro-iterations. As I said earlier, it shouldn't hurt.

Note: I advocate using this philosophy for plot points, not fine details. If there are logistical issues that you know you have to address (like the items on your Act One need-to-know list or your Act Three accounting list), don't rely on your memory alone. You're liable to forget what these issues are when the time comes to take care of them.

Instead, jot them down as they occur to you, and refer to them when needed (if you embrace iterative outlining, that would be mostly during, or after, stage 3).

An additional note: while updating this writing guide, I realized there is a way to use audio recording and still preserve the efficiency of the walkenwright method (in fact, you'd be even more efficient!). Here's what you do:

(1) Using a device of your choice, record audio *only* for the keeper micro-iteration from each of your walkenwright sessions.

(2) Transcribe this audio using software or a service.

If you're a dictation enthusiast, I bet this approach is music to your ears!

What about multiple-protagonist stories? Can I use the walkenwright method for them?

The walkenwright method is best suited for single-protagonist and dual-protagonist stories. All the same, it can be adapted for multiple-protagonist stories, with three or more protagonists—but it does require a bit of elbow grease.

That's because you have to treat each protagonist separately, and build an outline for each one individually (as if you were writing a single-protagonist story). To compose your starter outline, you'd weave together most (probably not all) of the plot points from each of these single-protagonist outlines.

To do so, first comb through your single-protagonist outlines, isolating the scenes that incorporate more than one protagonist. For example, in the outline told from Protagonist A's point of view, Protagonist A may've argued with Protagonist B and, within the same scene, cajoled Protagonist C. And in the outline told from Protagonist D's point of view, Protagonist D may've tried to kill Protagonist A.

Using these scenes as linchpins, logically fill in the plot points between them by plucking premade plot points from your single-protagonist outlines or generating new plot points, as needed.

You're laying down so many rules. I'm almost afraid to ask… what about music? Can I listen to music during my walkenwright sessions?

Ask yourself if listening to music will enable you to clearly hear your own voice.

There's your answer.

Do I really need to go on a genre fast?

You're not beholden to any of these suggestions. No one's going to be checking up on you. But if your output is sluggish, and you're dissatisfied with yourself because of it, then a radical change in tactics is probably necessary.

Also, if you're vehemently resistant to the idea of temporarily cutting out novels, social media, the nightly news, etc. from your life, it could be a sign that you're going to benefit the most by doing so.

The walkenwright method makes me nervous. Do you have alternatives?

The walkenwright method isn't for the faint of heart.

It takes a leap of faith; it is an act of courage.

Faith and courage usually result in reward—and this is no exception. For me, it's been the quickest and least agonizing way to complete an outline for a story.

Granted, it does take some getting used to. If you're nervous about it, take it for a test-drive when you've got nothing to lose, perhaps with a project that you've long since abandoned.

At the other end of the pressure spectrum, give the walkenwright method a spin when you're under a tight deadline and you *must* produce a finished outline...or else. A meeting with an editor, for instance. Or an unexpected, last-minute pitching opportunity.

After all that, if you and the walkenwright method just don't get along, try one of these nine alternatives:

(1) Snowplowing by Hal Ackerman

Starting with your core idea, you bulldoze or "snowplow" your way till the end—multiple times.

Sound familiar?

The walkenwright method was heavily inspired by the snowplow method, so the two share similarities. However, there's one key difference between them: with the snowplow method, you DO get to write everything down.

More details can be found in *How to Write Screenplays That Sell—The Ackerman Way*.

(2) Index Cards + The Board

With this method, you write down scenes on index cards, arrange them on a giant board, and then rearrange them until you are satisfied.

Many screenwriters use a variation of this technique, so it's described in different places. Blake Snyder's explanation in *Save the Cat* is one of the easiest to understand.

(3) John Truby's 22 Steps

Here, the structure of your story originates with your hero's psychological need ("a serious flaw that is hurting nobody but the hero") and his moral need (a flaw that harms other people). It ends with a revelation about his identity.

A full explanation of all the steps can be found in *The Anatomy of Story*.

(4) The Hero's Journey

This topic is a dense one. *The Writer's Journey* by Christopher Vogler makes it accessible to writers. With his guidelines, you'll build an outline by uniting Jungian archetypes with mythic structure.

When you're done, your outline may include such plot beats as:

- call to adventure
- meeting with the mentor
- crossing the threshold
- return with the elixir

(5) The Snowflake Method by Randy Ingermanson

Starting with your logline as a base, you expand it into "a full paragraph describing the story setup, major disasters, and ending." After that, you basically expand upon each sentence from this paragraph, so that they each have a paragraph of their own.

Then, you expand upon each of these paragraphs…and so on, and so forth.

More details can be found at Ingermanson's website (for the link, see no. 25 in the notes section at the end of this chapter) as well as in his book, *How to Write a Novel Using the Snowflake Method*.

PS: If you need help figuring out the disaster that ends Act Two, check out my writing guide *Trough of Hell*.

(6) The Phase Method by Lazette Gifford

Author Lazette Gifford has used this method to write "a 101,000-word book in 10 days." [26]

This is a quick summary of how she does it: she maps out her entire book in advance by describing it piecemeal, in phases (of about 20–50 words). Then, she expands those phases into tiny scenes (of about 200–400 words each; it depends on her target word count).

Phases, in case you were wondering, "bring the next set of lines—the next action—into focus…it can be clues to dialogue…or it might be a little bit of description."

You can find examples of specific phases (and how Gifford expanded them into mini-scenes) within issue no. 15 of *Vision: A Resource for Writers*. (For the link, refer to note no. 26.)

(7) D. C. Purk's Alternating Method

As I was working on updates to this writing guide, I stumbled across a comment made on scriptshadow.com by D. C. Purk. [27]

Although Purk accepts that outlining has its virtues, he feels that story characters get shortchanged in the process. So he devised an interesting solution.

Instead of outlining his story in one shot—or writing it all out in one shot—he *alternates* outlining with writing.

First, he outlines Act One. Next, instead of outlining the first half of Act Two (a.k.a. Act 2A), he writes Act One. Then he outlines Act 2A based on what he learned about his story and characters over the course of writing Act One. After that, he writes Act 2A. The same process is applied to the second half of Act Two (a.k.a. Act 2B) and, finally, Act Three.

As he put it, this enables a writer to:

> **Step away from your boring mechanical outline to put character and dialogue onto the page…While you're working your outline out, you're also getting to know your characters a little bit. How they talk, how they perceive the world, etc.**

Even though I've presented Purk's solution as an alternative to the walkenwright method, the two actually work well together.

To quickly spell it out, the process would look like this:

- Walkenwright up until the first-act break. (Follow the procedure described in chapter 15.)
- Write Act One.
- Walkenwright up until the midpoint.
- Write Act 2A.
- Walkenwright up until the trough of hell.

- Write Act 2B.
- Walkenwright through the resolution.
- Write Act Three.

Notably, this hybrid approach harnesses together the efficiency of outlining with the joy of writing—enabling both plotters and pantsers to balance productivity with personal satisfaction.

(8) The Evil Overlord Plotting Method by Teresa Nielsen Hayden

With this method, hatched by Tor editor Teresa Nielsen Hayden (insert evil-overlord-laughter sound effect here), you use randomly generated numbers to collect plot points from "various lovingly compiled cliché lists" on the internet. [28]

Connect these clichés together in an interesting (i.e. non-clichéd) way—and voila!—there's your outline.

Alas, the lists of clichés Hayden recommends reside on now-defunct websites. Happily, her own website will generate five random clichés for you. (See note no. 29 for the link.)

If you'd like more flexibility, you can pluck clichés from:

- an evil overlord cliché list, originating from musing on the clichés in Bond films, and compiled by Jack Butler (see note no. 30 for the link)
- an evil overlord cliché list, originating from musing on the clichés found in *Deep Space Nine*, and compiled by Peter Anspach (see note no. 31)

- a grand list of sci-fi clichés compiled by John VanSickle (see note no. 32)
- a grand list of fantasy clichés compiled by Teresa Dietzinger (see note no. 33)
- 100 movie clichés "that just won't die" compiled by Mark Pickavance for Den of Geek! (see note no. 34)

Two more points: Hayden suggests juicing up the plot with twists pulled from Murphy's Laws of Combat. (Different versions are available online. Search to find your favorite!) She recommends rolling a die to figure out how many laws to throw in.

Also, she cautions that "if you have one plot presented three ways, you have three plots. If you have three plots presented in one way, you have one plot."

If you're having trouble figuring out whether you're telling a story with one plot presented in three different ways (i.e. a story with an identity crisis) or a cohesive story with one plot, be sure to read Part II of *Solid Story Compass*, the next book in the Iterative Outlining series.

(9) Writing into the Dark by Dean Wesley Smith

This outline-free method is included for variety. With it, you only write one draft of your story.

Here's an overview of the process: start with a scene from your story's beginning that you can clearly visualize, and write forward from it for as long as you can. (Smith writes about 500–700 words.)

Then, loop backward, reading what you've written and making

adjustments as you see fit. When you reach the point where you stopped writing, write forward from there, and then loop backward again.

You can find more details in Smith's writing guide *Writing into the Dark*.

• • •

Keep in mind, the list above is meant to be a comprehensive set of *alternatives* to the walkenwright method.

Give it a shot first.

Odds are, you'll be amazed at how quickly it will enable you to dig up the bones belonging to your story.

With that exhortation, let's move on to the action steps for Part III!

ACTION STEP(S)

(23) Organize your notes from Parts I and II.

Prepare for your walkenwright sessions by collating together your notes from Parts I and II of this writing guide.

First, write out your logline from action step #12. Underneath it, write down your genre selection from action step #7.

Finally, describe these plot points from your structure code:

- opening image (from action step #16)
- first-act break (from action step #13)

- midpoint (from action step #17)
- trough (from action steps #18a–c or #20)
- climax (from action steps #19a–b or #20)
- resolution (from action steps #21a–b)

Collate your notes on a single sheet of paper or use the convenient worksheet available on my website.

To access it, just visit the link below:

➡ http://scribemeetsworld.com/wwp-worksheet/

(24) Conduct walkenwright session #1 and plot Act One, a.k.a. the beginning of your story.

Following the process described in chapter 15, fill in the plot points between the opening image of your story and its first-act break.

Note: You've picked your inciting incident based on your first-act break, and your opening image based on your inciting incident. Logically, when you plot out the events between the opening image and the first-act break, the inciting incident should make an appearance, without extra effort on your part.

It may not manifest itself in quite the same way (in some cases, it may be completely unrecognizable from what you chose in action step #15), but it should be there.

For your own peace of mind, however, once you've finished writing down your keeper micro-iteration, you might want to do a quick check and make sure an inciting incident, in some form, has been included.

(25) Conduct walkenwright session #2 and plot Act 2A, a.k.a. the first half of the middle of your story.

On the following day (for the sake of simplicity, let's say it's Tuesday), embark on your second walkenwright session.

To warm up, when you begin your walk, mentally rehearse either the last 4–5 (at a minimum) or all (the ideal) plot points from Act One, which you recorded during walkenwright session #1. Don't consult your notes. Go by memory alone.

Then, using the walkenwright method, fill in the plot points between the first-act break and the midpoint of your story.

(26) Conduct walkenwright session #3 and plot Act 2B, a.k.a. the second half of the middle of your story.

On Wednesday, begin your third walkenwright session. To warm up, mentally rehearse plot points from Act 2A, which you recorded during walkenwright session #2.

Then, using the walkenwright method, fill in the plot points between the midpoint of your story and its trough.

If you've become adept at combining multiple trough types together, you may find that Act 2B is already virtually complete.

Conduct a walkenwright session for Act 2B anyway.

Since you've now plotted out Act 2A, you have greater insight into the inner workings of your story. This may guide you toward an Act 2B that's significantly different than what you originally envisioned.

(27) Conduct walkenwright session #4 and plot Act Three, a.k.a. the end of your story.

On Thursday, it's time for your fourth walkenwright session—the home stretch. To warm up, mentally rehearse plot points from Act 2B, which you recorded during walkenwright session #3.

Afterward, use the walkenwright method to take your story from the trough through the climax; and then from the climax through the resolution.

(28) Conduct walkenwright session #5 (this is optional) and celebrate (this is not).

On Friday, take it from the top!

In one monster walkenwright session, fill in the plot points from the opening image of your story through its resolution.

This is gonna be a challenge. In particular, it puts a strain on your short-term memory.

Only take this step if you're up for it.

Finally, celebrate your achievement. You have an outline of your entire story in your hands. There's still some fine-tuning to do (all your keeper micro-iterations have to be integrated together), but don't worry about that tonight.

Instead, savor your success and give yourself a treat. You earned it!

NOTES FOR PART III

Chapter 16

7. Mason Currey, "Daily Rituals," Culturebox, *Slate*, April 25, 2013, http://www.slate.com/articles/arts/culturebox/features/2013/daily_rituals/tchaikovsky_beethoven_mahler_they_all_loved_taking_long_daily_walks.html.

8. Dan Mitchell, "Silicon Valley's Different Kind of Power Walk," *Fortune*, November 15, 2011, http://fortune.com/2011/11/15/silicon-valleys-different-kind-of-power-walk/.

9. Ferris Jabr, "Why Walking Helps Us Think," Elements, *New Yorker*, September 3, 2014, http://www.newyorker.com/tech/elements/walking-helps-us-think.

10. Marily Oppezzo and Daniel L. Schwartz, "Give Your Ideas Some Legs: The Positive Effect of Walking on Creative Thinking," *Journal of Experimental Psychology: Learning, Memory, and Cognition* 40, no. 4 (2014): 1142–1152, doi:10.1037/a0036577.

11. Gretchen Reynolds, "Want to Be More Creative? Take a Walk," *New York Times* (Well blog), April 30, 2014, http://well.blogs.nytimes.com/2014/04/30/want-to-be-more-creative-take-a-walk/.

12. See note no. 7.

Chapter 17

13. Leslie Berlin, "We'll Fill This Space, But First a Nap,"

New York Times, September 28, 2008, http://www.nytimes.com/2008/09/28/technology/28proto.html.

14. Ut Na Sio, Padraic Monaghan, and Tom Ormerod, "Sleep on It, But Only If It Is Difficult: Effects of Sleep on Problem Solving," *Memory & Cognition* 41, no. 2 (2013): 159–166, doi:10.3758/s13421-012-0256-7.

15. See note no. 13.

16. Stacy Conradt, "Creative Breakthroughs That Came During Sleep," *Atlantic*, October 12, 2012, http://www.theatlantic.com/health/archive/2012/10/creative-breakthroughs-that-came-during-sleep/263562/.

17. Stacey Anderson, "When Keith Richards Wrote '(I Can't Get No) Satisfaction' in His Sleep," *Rolling Stone*, May 9, 2011, http://www.rollingstone.com/music/news/when-keith-richards-wrote-i-cant-get-no-satisfaction-in-his-sleep-20110509.

18. See note no. 16.

19. Denise J. Cai et al., "REM, Not Incubation, Improves Creativity by Priming Associative Networks," *Proceedings of the National Academy of Sciences (PNAS)* 106, no. 25 (2009): 10130–10134, doi:10.1073/pnas.0900271106.

20. James Randerson, "Sleep Scientists Discount Sheep," *New Scientist*, January 23, 2002, https://www.newscientist.com/article/dn1831-sleep-scientists-discount-sheep/.

21. Joseph Mercola, "Tips and Tricks to Help You Fall Asleep Faster," February 16, 2017, http://articles.mercola.com/sites/articles/archive/2017/02/16/tips-tricks-fall-asleep-faster.aspx.

22. Michael Connelly, "What I Did on My Summer Vacation," accessed May 20, 2018, http://michaelconnelly.com/otherwords/summer/.

Chapter 18

23. May Wong, "Stanford Study Finds Walking Improves Creativity," Stanford University press release, April 24, 2014, http://news.stanford.edu/news/2014/april/walking-vs-sitting-042414.html.

24. See note no. 10.

25. Randy Ingermanson, "The Snowflake Method for Designing a Novel," accessed May 20, 2018, http://www.advancedfictionwriting.com/articles/snowflake-method/.

26. Lazette Gifford, "It's Just a Phase," *Vision: A Resource for Writers*, no. 15 (2003), http://fmwriters.com/Visionback/Index.htm.

27. D. C. Purk, March 30, 2017 (5:24 p.m.), comment on Carson Reeves, "How to Write a Script Without an Outline," *Scriptshadow* (blog), March 30, 2017, http://scriptshadow.net/how-to-write-a-script-without-an-outline/.

28. Teresa Nielsen Hayden, "The Evil Overlord Devises a Plot," Viable Paradise Science Fiction and Fantasy Writers' Workshop, accessed February 21, 2012, http://www.sff.net/paradise/plottricks.htm (site discontinued).

29. Teresa Nielsen Hayden, "Random Plot Generator," accessed May 20, 2018, http://www.nielsenhayden.com/overlord/.

30. Jack Butler, "The Evil Overlord List," accessed May 20, 2018, http://legendspbem.angelfire.com/eviloverlordlist.html.

31. Peter Anspach, "The Top 100 Things I'd Do If I Ever Became an Evil Overlord," accessed May 20, 2018, http://www.eviloverlord.com/lists/overlord.html.

32. John VanSickle, "The Grand List of Overused Science Fiction Clichés," *Dragon Writing Prompts* (blog), February 17, 2007, http://dragonwritingprompts.blogspot.com/2007/02/grand-list-of-overused-science-fiction.html.

33. Teresa Dietzinger, "The Not-So-Grand List of Overused Fantasy Clichés," *Dragon Writing Prompts* (blog), September 29, 2007, http://dragonwritingprompts.blogspot.com/2007/09/not-so-grand-list-of-overused-fantasy.html.

34. Mark Pickavance, "100 Movie Clichés That Just Won't Die…" *Den of Geek!* (blog), June 1, 2009, http://denofgeek.com/movies/14432/100-movie-clichés-that-just-won't-die…

- PART IV -

WRAPPING UP

JUST AS YOU MUST TIE UP LOOSE ENDS BY THE END OF YOUR screenplay or novel, we must do the same here.

In these final chapters, we will address matters that will make both your starter outline and your reading experience (of this writing guide) complete.

More specifically, we'll cover:

- the finishing touches that need be applied to your starter outline
- a convenient checklist of all the action steps that comprise stage 1 of iterative outlining
- a concluding note on the flexibility of the process

Let's get on with it, shall we?

- chapter nineteen -

APPLYING THE FINISHING TOUCHES TO YOUR STARTER OUTLINE

ALTHOUGH EFFECTIVE, THE WALKENWRIGHT method isn't perfect.

As mentioned previously, when you're digging up story bones, you may collect bones that belong to another story altogether. (Perhaps one you will write at another time.)

In addition, the bones that do belong to your current project are in an imperfect state. They still have dirt clinging to them that needs to be cleared away. Calcified deposits may've become encrusted to their surface, and must be removed, before you can get a sense of their true shape. Tiny (sometimes large) chips must be filled in.

Finally, after all of this restoration, you must assemble these bones together.

This grand undertaking largely falls under the purview of stages 2 (say what you mean) and 3 (say it well) of iterative outlining. Yet, a small part of it falls within the scope of stage 1, and that is the topic of this chapter, which is composed solely of action steps.

First, we will take care of the action steps that must be completed to finalize your starter outline. Afterward, we'll look at some optional action steps. In fact, to maximize your efficiency, it's better to complete these optional action steps during stages 2 and 3 of iterative outlining.

Nevertheless, I include them in this chapter in case you don't advance on to stages 2 and 3, and instead, launch your rough draft based on your stage 1 starter outline. If you do (as recommended) hold off on completing the optional action steps, make a note to yourself to revisit them at a later point in your writing process.

ACTION STEP(S)

(29) Assemble a full outline from your keeper micro-iterations.

Take out all of your keeper micro-iterations. Unless you deviated from the action steps at the end of chapter 18, you should have four of them (plus a fifth, if you conducted a monster walkenwright session per action step #28; ignore the fifth for the time being).

In a single document, type (or copy and paste) each set of plot points according to order—starting with Act One (from walkenwright session #1), moving on to Act 2A (from walkenwright session #2) and Act 2B (from walkenwright session #3), and finally ending with Act Three (from walkenwright session #4).

This is the rough cut of your starter outline.

If you conducted a monster walkenwright session, consult your notes from it now. Compare them to the starter outline you just assembled. Are there deviations? Do you like them?

If so, incorporate them into your starter outline and make adjustments as necessary.

(30) Review plot point ideas outside the scope of each day's walkenwright session.

Recall that on each walkenwright session (besides the first), you mentally rehearsed plot points from the previous day's session. Your rehearsal may've resulted in variation (e.g. on Day 2, while rehearsing, you came up with a variation to Day 1's keeper micro-iteration, and you brainstormed ideas for Day 2's plot points based on this variation).

Examine such variations now. When you insert them into their appropriate place (in this case, the variation was to Day 1's keeper micro-iteration, which means it'd have to be inserted into Act One), what kind of ripple effects do they cause? Make changes to your starter outline as needed.

Next, take a look at any ideas you got for "future" plot points (e.g. when you wrote down your keeper micro-iteration on Day 2, you may've gotten ideas for Day 3). Did you actually use those ideas on Day 3? Or did you forget about them by the time Day 3's walkenwright session rolled around?

If you did forget about them—and you'd like to integrate them into your outline—do so now.

(31) Evaluate your midpoint fulcrums.

In action step #17, you were supposed to choose one midpoint fulcrum to work with. However, your story may've lent itself to more than one fulcrum. Now's the time to take these other fulcrums into account.

For the sake of illustration, let's say you're writing a romantic thriller. This genre usually pairs together an antagonist-aha midpoint with a bond builder.

You conducted your walkenwright sessions based on the antagonist-aha midpoint. Now, examine your starter outline to see how well you addressed the bond builder.

More than likely, you've taken care of it by default. Still, look for opportunities to accentuate this midpoint, so that the budding relationship between the hero and heroine is accorded its due.

If you like, you can outline your story again—this time, brainstorming ideas using the bond builder as your midpoint fulcrum (as opposed to the antagonist aha). You could conduct walkenwright sessions just for the middle (Acts 2A and 2B), or for your entire story, or somewhere in between. Refine your starter outline in light of any new discoveries you make.

It's extra work, sure, but it might yield a gold nugget that really brings your story together. The choice (whether to accentuate what you've got or outline your story all over again) is yours.

The same can't be said if your story lends itself to two midpoints that can't be reconciled together (like the tide turner and the manifest midpoint, for instance). This isn't an optional step; you have to outline your story again. (I did warn you about this in chapter 11!)

So, if hypothetically, you built your starter outline using the tide-turner midpoint, now you have to conduct your walkenwright sessions using the manifest midpoint as your fulcrum. (This should be easier to do now that you have greater insight into your story.) It may also necessitate modifications to your trough and climax.

Which version of your story do you like better? Which one makes you feel fired up to write? That's the one you should proceed with.

If you opt for the alternative choice (in this case, the manifest midpoint), make sure to revisit action steps #29 and #30 before moving on.

On the off chance that you have three discrete midpoint fulcrums that can't be used in conjunction with one another, follow the same procedure. Outline your story using the third fulcrum option, compare this outline to the others, choose the version you like best, and proceed accordingly.

OPTIONAL ACTION STEPS

(32) Expand the time frame (potentially).

In action step #2, you took care of the S, M, and A of your

protagonist's SMART goal. Take a moment to reflect on the R (realistic) and T (time-bound) aspects of his goal and how they interact with each other.

Contracting the time frame is a great way to heighten tension. Despite this, you may have to expand the time frame for the sake of realism.

For example, in an action movie, your hero may need to spend more time under his mentor's tutelage in order to make your hero's transformation into a warrior more believable. In a romance, your hero may need more time (and, correspondingly, must endure more ordeals) in order to evolve into someone worthy of the heroine's love.

(33) Review your need-to-know and accounting lists.

In action step #14, you wrote down a list of things you anticipated audiences would need to know (in Act One) in order to understand and care about later events.

During your first walkenwright session, you probably included many of these items without even thinking about it—but not all. Integrate whatever you omitted (and which still bears relevance) into your starter outline.

Next, review your list of things that need to be accounted for by the end of your story (from action step #22). Items like subplots, red herrings, setups, etc. As you did with your need-to-know list, integrate these into your starter outline (if not there, already).

If you're unable to tie up these loose ends to your satisfaction, consult your seed bank (see action step #34, below). I've found this will often yield a wonderful solution.

(34) Inspect your seed bank.

Review all the ideas that you set aside in your seed bank. Odds are, you've already incorporated a fair share of these seeds into your outline. (Not because you forcefully crowbarred them into your story, but because they came to you, unbidden, during the development process.)

Examine what remains.

Some you'll be able to use straight out, and when you add them to your starter outline, it'll really start to sizzle!

Some won't be usable, as is, at all. They just don't belong in your story. Not anymore. But, with modification, these story seeds may be the perfect way to solve a thorny plot problem or address a logistical issue from your accounting list.

Scrutinize them carefully!

(35) Discover and/or refine your story's theme.

If you didn't start with a theme-based story kernel, now's the time to figure out your theme. Comb through your plot points. Pay special attention to your protagonist's most momentous choices. What do they say about life—and how to live it?

If you started with a theme-based story kernel, then you already know what theme you wanted your story to convey.

In either case, review your starter outline to see if it successfully conveys your theme. You may need to accentuate your theme in some areas, and play it down in others.

On that note, the fork in the road and the closing image are two great places to accentuate theme, which brings me to…

(36) Define the fork in the road and your closing image.

Look closely at the middle of your story, right around the midpoint and the first half of Act 2B. Does your protagonist make a tough choice that reflects your theme?

If not, can you find a way to build in a fork, i.e. put your protagonist in a position where he has to make this kind of choice?

Now, examine your first and last few plot points. Do they evoke any images that reflect your theme? If so, end your story with this image…unless you have a better image in mind (perhaps one that sets up a sequel!).

Note: You might not be able to complete this action step until you write your rough draft. Even then, don't stress it. Remember, although the fork and the closing image can greatly enhance your story, they are the least essential of the essential plot points.

(37) Worldbuild away!

At this point, you know a lot more about your story than when you established its setting in action step #8.

If necessary, you can dedicate your energy toward building up the areas of your story world that need it the most…and not fritter away your energy on areas that simply aren't relevant. (Unless, of course, worldbuilding is the most fun for you. Then have at it!)

Include backstories here, too. This is the time to figure out why your hero and heroine are, for instance, so emotionally guarded or reluctant to embrace their talents.

- chapter twenty -

YOUR CONVENIENT STARTER OUTLINE CHECKLIST

WHEN YOU'RE READY TO GENERATE YOUR OWN starter outline, it's helpful to have a list of all the action steps in one place.

For easy reference, you can find one in this chapter. In addition, a convenient, printable checklist of action steps can be found on my website, at the following link:

➡ http://scribemeetsworld.com/outline-checklist/

To avoid unnecessary redundancy, the steps don't include explanatory descriptions. If you need further clarification, you can always consult the relevant chapter in this book.

PART I: POPPING THE STORY KERNEL

- ☐ (1) Isolate your story kernel (situation-, character-, or theme-based).
- ☐ (2) Design your SMART goal and the protagonist who will pursue it. (S – specific, M – measurable, A – actionable, R – realistic, and T – time-bound.)
- ☐ (3a) Create the main antagonist of your story.
- ☐ (3b) Refine your protagonist accordingly.
- ☐ (4) Tackle your credibility strategy (this assumes your protagonist achieves victory).
- ☐ (5) Create an additional antagonist, if necessary (e.g. if you're writing a plot with a love triangle).
- ☐ (6) Determine your story stakes.
- ☐ (7) Cast your plot into a genre mold.
- ☐ (8) Settle on a setting (place, time, and season).
- ☐ (9) List all of your story's intrinsic hooks (setting, character, origin of material, tone, title, and irony).
- ☐ (10) Using one of the five irony combinations from chapter 6 (or one of your choice), amplify your story idea's quotient of irony.
- ☐ (11) Evaluate the hooks in your story, together, as a group.
- ☐ (12) Using the template from chapter 7, summarize your story in one sentence (the logline).

PART II: CRACKING YOUR STORY CODE

- ☐ (13) Determine the first-act break.

- [ ] (14) Figure out what goes onto your need-to-know list.
- [ ] (15) Working backward from the first-act break, choose an inciting incident.
- [ ] (16) Find your opening image, i.e. your point of entry into your story.
- [ ] (17) From the eight midpoint fulcrums listed in chapter 11, choose one to build the middle of your story around.
- [ ] (18a) From the master list in chapter 12, pick an obvious candidate for your trough.
- [ ] (18b) Working backward from a random trough type, find a way to fit it into your story's framework.
- [ ] (18c) Combine the trough types from action steps #18a and #18b.
- [ ] (19a) Briefly describe the climax of your story.
- [ ] (19b) Incorporate an element of momentousness (i.e. setting, urgency, or choice) into the climax.
- [ ] (20) Analyze the climax's compatibility with the trough.
- [ ] (21a) Determine your story's resolution (happy, tragic, or bittersweet).
- [ ] (21b) Designate a hallmark of change.
- [ ] (22) Get a jumpstart on your accounting.

PART III: EXCAVATING STORY FOSSILS

- [ ] (23) Organize your notes from Parts I and II (i.e. logline, genre, opening image, first-act break, midpoint, trough, climax, and resolution). If you wish, use this convenient worksheet, which is available on my website:

  http://scribemeetsworld.com/wwp-worksheet/

- ☐ (24) Following the instructions from chapter 15, conduct walkenwright session #1 and plot Act One, a.k.a. the beginning of your story.
- ☐ (25) Conduct walkenwright session #2 and plot Act 2A, a.k.a. the first half of the middle of your story.
- ☐ (26) Conduct walkenwright session #3 and plot Act 2B, a.k.a. the second half of the middle of your story.
- ☐ (27) Conduct walkenwright session #4 and plot Act Three, a.k.a. the end of your story.
- ☐ (28) Conduct walkenwright session #5 (this is optional) and celebrate (this is not).

PART IV: WRAPPING UP

- ☐ (29) Assemble a full outline from the keeper micro-iteration from each of your walkenwright sessions.
- ☐ (30) Review plot point ideas outside the scope of each day's walkenwright session.
- ☐ (31) Evaluate your midpoint fulcrums.

OPTIONAL ACTION STEPS

- ☐ (32) Expand the time frame (potentially).
- ☐ (33) Review your need-to-know and accounting lists.
- ☐ (34) Inspect your seed bank.
- ☐ (35) Discover and/or refine your story's theme.
- ☐ (36) Define the fork in the road and your closing image.
- ☐ (37) Worldbuild away!

- chapter twenty-one -

THE METHOD, AT YOUR SERVICE

LET'S BE CLEAR.

Your starter outline is a flexible creature.

It's not set in stone. You're not beholden to it.

If you embrace iterative outlining, by definition, your starter outline will evolve into something different as you progress through stages 2 and 3.

Even if you don't, even if you bypass these stages and plunge into your rough draft right away, in all likelihood, you'll deviate from your starter outline.

That's because new ideas will come to you as you speed through your draft. This outcome doesn't render your starter outline useless. On the contrary.

Your starter outline gave you the raw material that led you to these new ideas. In addition, since you already plotted out your story in advance, you'll be in a stronger position to decide whether these ideas are worth pursuing…or not, as the case may be.

Likewise, the method of generating your starter outline is flexible.

You're not beholden to it either.

Sure, it's been presented as a step-by-step system. In the beginning, that will be a virtue, something you find reassuring.

However, you're unlikely to use the same method for your seventh screenplay or tenth novel that you used for your second.

Eventually, following the full program—popping the story kernel, cracking the structural code, and digging up your story bones—might seem too rigid. Then, you'll probably deviate from the prescribed action steps.

You may add techniques that you learned from another writer, or tricks that you've discovered yourself.

You may take the steps to extremes, dividing each one further still. You may implement them in a different sequence. You may discard steps wholesale.

Over time, the method you follow might not even be recognizable as the one described in this book.

As even more time passes, the process will become so instinctive, that you might not consult an action plan at all.

Frankly, the method you use doesn't really matter—as long as you get reliable results.

Just remember...

...if you get stuck...

...if you have to resume writing after a long period of inactivity...

...if you have loads of free time and want to maximize your efficiency...

...in whatever circumstance you find yourself, you have a panic-free path to take you from idea to outline.

It's right here, waiting for you, when you need it.

Best of luck!

I wish you much success on your storytelling journey.

NOTES

A Letter For You, Fellow Scribe

Dear scribe,

Thank you so much for reading *Sizzling Story Outlines*.

Like my other writing guides, it's the result of spending years analyzing movies, screenplays, and novels to see why some stories are so gripping...while others are easy to walk away from.

I dedicated myself to this multi-year quest because I struggled to develop my story ideas in a way that would yield the gimme-all-the-feels experience I found in the stories I loved.

In fact, I struggled so much with plotting (as well as with several imiting beliefs) that I gave up on my writing dream and almost became a lawyer. *Twice.*

Anyway, during my quest, I initially focused on story structure because I knew it generated the up-and-down rhythm that keeps readers engaged from beginning to end.

Later, I realized another storytelling ingredient was also vital to creating reader "glue." From chapter 4 of this book, you know what it is too: the stakes.

To level up your writing game, you really need to master both structure *and* stakes. That's why I've created resources on these topics for novelists and screenwriters like yourself.

It's my wish that these resources will help you to hold fast to your writing dream—even when life tells you to let go.

While you can find more details about these resources on the following pages, I wanted to mention one of them here: the Story Stake Cheat Sheet.

It gives you a convenient list of 11 types of story stakes (+ definitions) so it'll be a breeze to pick the perfect set of stakes for your next novel or screenplay.

Please visit the link below to download the cheat sheet for free:

http://scribemeetsworld.com/stakes-cheat-sheet/

I believe in you,

H. R. D'Costa (a.k.a. HRD)
Scribe Meets World

PS: After you download the cheat sheet, would you take a second to recommend *Sizzling Story Outlines* to a writing buddy of yours who's struggling with plotting a story?

It'd be a triple-win situation.

Your friend would win because he or she would get an outlining method that can be used by both plotters and pantsers; you'd win due to the good karma you'd accrue; and I'd win because I'd be fulfilling my mission to help more people hold fast to their writing dreams :)

SOLID
STORY COMPASS
iterative outlining #2

How to Be Your Own Developmental Editor or Script Consultant, Stop Second-Guessing Your Storytelling Decisions, and Prevent Inconsistencies from Incurring Reader Wrath

You did it.

You finished your screenplay or novel. Can we say dance party?

But after you're done celebrating, your feeling of elation—pfft!—vanishes.

That's because you took a closer look at your draft.

Sure, you've got pages filled with words. Unfortunately, those pages don't add up to a coherent story. Truth is, your draft is all over the place.

Basically, there's a gap (OK, sometimes, it's more like a chasm) between the story in your head...and the one you've actually penned to paper.

While you realize that something's wrong, you can't pinpoint exactly what it is...which means you can't fix it.

Now, a talented developmental editor or script consultant could help you out. They could figure out what's wrong, what's weak, and what's not working—and dish out the fixes.

If you had a stack of cash lying around, you'd hire a pro like that in a jiffy. But at the moment, you don't. So...until then, what can you do?

You can't leave things as they are. That'll just trigger brutal coverage or scathing reviews. Uhm, no thanks.

Instead, you must view your story with more objectivity than you're used to. You must learn how to do a big-picture edit of your screenplay or novel on your own.

Does that sound scary?

Don't worry. This writing guide will show you what to do. Through step-by-step instructions, you'll:

- smooth out your plot and avoid comments like "it was all over the place" or "it unraveled quickly"
- ensure that audiences invest in your protagonist—instead of in another character (which causes the kind of confusion that generates hostile reviews)
- maximize genre's ability to be your personal rainmaker
- tackle 5 types of tonal inconsistencies (which, despite being minor, can lead to major disgruntlement)
- use 6 tools to extract potential themes from your story (after which, you'll polish one of these themes until it shines)

Buy *Solid Story Compass* now and become your own developmental editor or script consultant today!

To learn where you can buy this writing guide, please visit:

http://scribemeetsworld.com/compass/

SPARKLING STORY DRAFTS
iterative outlining #3

How to Outline Your Way Toward Cleaner Rough Drafts, Reduce Your Revision Time, and Get a First-Rate Screenplay or Novel onto the Marketplace—Faster

More, more, more.

Whether screenwriter or novelist, the more you write, the more money you're likely to earn.

The more market-ready scripts you have, the more enticing you'll be to an agent. The more novels you publish, the more you'll boost your discoverability.

But to produce more, you need more time. That's because you've got to juggle a lot (job responsibilities, a family, self-care) besides writing—and there are only 24 hours in the day.

So, is it possible to achieve your writing goals without burning out?

Yes. But to do so, you need to write quicker, you need to write better—the first time around. How? By outlining your story in advance.

This will boost your productivity because:

(1) You'll know where your story is headed, so you'll start strong—and stay strong (instead of petering out halfway through your story).

(2) Compared to a full draft, there's less material to review so it's easier to identify—and fix—problem spots.

(3) You won't waste time perfecting scenes that'll ultimately have to be deleted. This should reduce your revision time (by months, potentially).

But to maximize your efficiency when writing your novel or script, you need a systematic way to analyze your outline and improve your story.

That's what this writing guide will teach you, step by step. With it, you'll:

- zap episodic plots with a secret ingredient (if you're using the hero's journey to plot, this is a must-have)
- pump up your story structure so it delivers maximum entertainment value
- apply a psychology trick to your genre goods to make your story even more addictive
- integrate subplots in a way that enhances the main plot
- sidestep sluggish pacing
- achieve the ideal cast size, so that audiences can easily keep track of what's going on, while still remaining emotionally involved in the action
- run through 4 quick tests to prevent dull or useless scenes from cluttering up your story

Buy *Sparkling Story Drafts* now and usher in an era of faster writing, fewer edits, and first-rate story quality!

> An essential roadmap for both new and veteran writers.
>
> ~ Elizabeth Spann Craig, author of 25+ cozy mysteries (including the bestselling Myrtle Clover series) and award-winning blogger

To learn where you can buy this writing guide, please visit:

http://scribemeetsworld.com/draft/

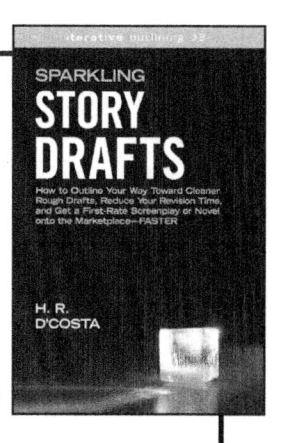

STORY STAKES

Your #1 Writing Skills Strategy to Produce a Page-Turner That Transforms Readers into Raving Fans of Your Screenplay or Novel

Wouldn't it be great if readers stayed up all night to finish your screenplay or novel?

When these readers are done with your story, they won't quickly forget about it and reach for another spec script or novel in their TBR pile.

Nope. Not after such an intense emotional experience like that. Instead, they'll transform into raving fans who will tell everyone they know about your work.

That's how you get onto Hollywood's radar and eventually make the big spec sale. That's how you get the word-of-mouth recommendations that propel a novel to the top of the bestseller lists.

It's how you finally achieve your writing dreams.

Sounds nice, right? But how do you make it happen? How do you keep readers glued to your screenplay or novel?

A likeable hero and a high-concept premise only go so far. They entice readers to give your story a chance, but they don't keep readers engaged till the very end.

To accomplish this, you need something more: story stakes.

Because of the stakes, your protagonist can't walk away from his problem. As a result, readers won't be able to walk away from your story.

See, when stakes are in play, readers wonder whether your protagonist will succeed or fail at his goal. Then, they worry about him. Then, they're under tension.

To relieve this tension, they must stay up all night and finish your story—and when they have, they'll rave about the amazing page-turner they couldn't put down. They'll rave about **you**.

Master story stakes and you can eclipse the competition. This book will show you how. Specifically, you'll learn about:

- 11 types of story stakes which increase tension and reader engagement
- 8 modulating factors which affect the emotional impact of the stakes
- specific strategies to raise the stakes (even when they're already high!)
- how to use stakes to craft a premise with more commercial appeal

Buy *Story Stakes* today and take a step closer toward enthralled readers, raving fans, and killer sales!

> H. R. D'Costa shows writers how to layer stakes, one on top of another, blending them into a compelling tangle from which the hero—and the reader—cannot escape. This is now one of my favorite go-to guides on writing.
>
> ~ Debbie Burke, author of the thrillers *Instrument of the Devil* (a Kindle Scout and Zebulon Award winner) and *Stalking Midas*

To learn where you can buy this writing guide, please visit:

http://scribemeetsworld.com/stakes/

Story Structure Essentials series

"Deep dive" writing guides to help you craft novels and screenplays that readers can't put down

Part II of *Sizzling Story Outlines* covered the basics of story structure. It got your feet wet. Do you want to go deep-sea diving and learn how to execute each structural turning point in the most gripping way possible?

Then you must check out the writing guides in the Story Structure Essentials series:

INCITING INCIDENT
How to Begin Your Screenplay or Novel and Captivate Audiences Right Away
(While Accomplishing Your Long-Term Plotting Goals)

REVISED & EXPANDED edition

H. R. D'COSTA
STORY STRUCTURE essentials

MIDPOINT MAGIC
How to Swing Your Screenplay or Novel in a New Direction and Say Good-Bye to Sagging Story Middles That Put Audiences to Sleep

H. R. D'COSTA
STORY STRUCTURE essentials

TROUGH OF HELL
How to Wrap Up the Middle of Your Story with MAXIMUM IMPACT

H. R. D'COSTA
STORY STRUCTURE essentials

STORY CLIMAX
How to Avoid Disappointed Audiences and Craft a Screenplay or Novel Climax That THRILLS & DELIGHTS

H. R. D'COSTA
STORY STRUCTURE essentials

These are some of the best books I've read about writing. I wish I found them before! My plotting process is no longer scattered, I don't cycle back and forth because I forgot something or things don't work.

~ Anna Flakk, author of the urban-fantasy novel *A Wicked Chance*

To learn more, please visit:

http://scribemeetsworld.com/books/

INCITING INCIDENT
Story Structure Essentials

How to Begin Your Screenplay or Novel and Captivate Audiences Right Away (While Accomplishing Your Long-Term Plotting Goals)

Beginnings are agonizing to write.

So much is at stake.

If you start your novel or screenplay in the wrong place, if it's boring or bogged down by exposition, audiences will abandon it right then and there.

They're not going to read further to see if your story gets better down the road. They don't have to.

Whether a studio executive, agent, or bookworm, they're spoiled for choice.

They can make quick judgment calls, instantly forsaking your story for one that grabs them right away.

In other words, a well-written beginning helps you sell your story. But…it has to do more than that. It also has to set up your plot.

Unfortunately, setting your pieces in place (especially the character stuff) tends to be slow. It doesn't tend to grab audiences.

At the same time, it doesn't do you much good to grab audiences at the beginning…only to lose them later on because they've become confused or haven't really connected with your characters.

This is the marketing-plotting conundrum. And boy is it a doozy.

Happily, this "deep dive" writing guide will show you how to navigate it with confidence.

Do you want to know:

- whether your story beginning has the kind of pacing and momentum that will attract audiences…or repel them?
- how much "everyday" world to include before the inciting incident (plus 5 tips to make your protagonist's everyday world more interesting)?
- how to fix a story that starts too fast (rather than too slow)?
- 8 ways to start your novel or screenplay (and why some "controversial" beginnings might not be as bad as you believe)?
- an easy fix to organically weave in exposition and avoid those "as you know" conversations that drive audiences crazy?

Then *Inciting Incident* is the writing guide you should read right now.

> I loved *Inciting Incident*. It was so great that this morning I bought *Midpoint Magic*. My plan is to buy all the books in the Story Structure Essentials series.
>
> ~ Sharon Wray, author of the Amazon bestselling Deadly Force romantic-suspense series

Buy *Inciting Incident* today and learn how to craft a masterful story beginning that (a) hits readers' buy buttons *and* (b) gets your plotting pieces in place!

http://scribemeetsworld.com/inciting/

FINISH THAT DRAFT*
TODAY.
* and make it awesome!

By following the instructions in Part II of *Sizzling Story Outlines*, you've already cracked your story's structure.

So why invest in another structure resource like my online course Smarter Story Structure? Well...it enables you to explore story structure further, without spending a lot of time.

You see, I took the best takeaways from the Story Structure Essentials series (these are "deep dive" writing guides that, together, total over 250,000 words)—as well as from *Story Stakes* and *Sparkling Story Drafts*—and condensed them into 5 modules that you can binge on in a weekend.

In others words, the course is your shortcut to creating stories that are good enough to keep readers *hooked*.

Here's a sampling of what you'll receive when you purchase the course:

- page numbers to place your inciting incident so you know your story doesn't start too slowly
- a surefire way to detect whether your novel or screenplay only gains traction halfway through (a common problem)
- more tips on how to execute the "all is lost" moment with skill
- instructions on how to craft an epically long climax that will dazzle audiences (rather than fizzling out and delivering a wimpy ending)
- advice on how to increase the odds that your resolution will net you more sales

Still wondering whether the course is right for you? OK, let me ask:

- Do you have an AMAZING story idea that the marketplace would gobble up, so you want to bang out a draft ASAP?
- Do you want a quick refresher on structure before you dive into each of your writing projects? (This is especially valuable if your writing schedule is erratic.)
- Do you learn better with visuals and video?
- Do you enjoy plotting with worksheets and reinforcing your knowledge with writing exercises?

Then Smarter Story Structure is the online writing course you've been looking for.

> This course, Smarter Story Structure, is fantastic & spot-on. For me, it's been a series of mini-light bulbs popping off along the way, and I can't thank you enough for your insight and clarity.
>
> ~ James Caffery, Quarterfinalist in the WeScreenPlay Pilot Competition (2018)
>
> I love, love, love this course. It will be such a time (and mistake) saver.
>
> ~ Ariadne S

Enroll now and become a story structure ninja from the comfort of your own home:

HTTP://SCRIBEMEETSWORLD.COM/3AS/

WRITE YOUR NOVEL OR SCREENPLAY NOW.

Would you like to finally get your book or movie idea out of your head and onto paper...and:

- stop stifling your creativity?
- make the leap from entertainment consumer to creator?
- no longer let excuses hold you back from pursuing your writing dream?

Then **UNLOCK YOUR INNER WRITER** is perfect for you.

This 12-week coaching program will enable you to go from dreaming about writing a novel or screenplay to having done it!

It's a good fit for you if you value having:

- a clear, step-by-step plan to finish a project
- periodic feedback so you know you're on the right track
- an accountability partner to help you follow through on your intentions and stay the course, despite your busy schedule
- encouragement and support along the way so that, despite the ups and downs of being creative, you don't lose sight of how awesome you are

Learn more about this hands-on, personalized coaching program:

http://scribemeetsworld.com/unlocked/

PREFER TO GO DIY?

You have the dream to write a screenplay. But you're finding it tough to take action.

Whether you're looking to write your first screenplay (ever) or write your first screenplay draft (more easily), you *can* end your writing sessions with a big smile because of all the pages you got written.

How? Through the step-by-step process outlined in my writing guide *How to Write a Screenplay Now*.

Wanna know more? Here's a brief sampling of what you'll learn with this screenwriting book:

- how to carve out an hour of time to write each day (& how to defend that time without feeling guilty)
- the best way to stop feeling intimidated by the format for writing a screenplay
- how to break your story's structure, get to know your characters & conduct research without getting stuck in procrastination mode
- 13 unusual ways to subdue the voice inside your head that tells you that your writing's no good
- a game plan for revising your draft, after it's done

Buy *How to Write a Screenplay Now*, get started on your screenplay today...and unleash your full writing potential!

http://scribemeetsworld.com/screenplay-now/

About the Author

A graduate of Brown University, H. R. D'Costa almost became a lawyer—twice—because it seemed easier and less scary than doing what she really wanted: to be a writer.

That's why she's on a mission to create mindset and plotting resources that will enable novelists and screenwriters to hold fast to their writing dreams…even when life tells them to let go.

For inspiration; practical writing tips; and her popular resource, the Ultimate Story Structure Worksheet (which has been downloaded over 37,000 times by writers from around the world), she invites you to visit her website scribemeetsworld.com.

> Your books were the key for me to finish my drafts. I'm a beginner, but you made me feel capable of writing the stories I want to share, with confidence. I don't have enough words to thank you! You are one of the reasons for me to reach my dream.
>
> ~ C. J. Lamb, urban-fantasy author

> The clarity of your approach is refreshing, and you make all this feel so approachable.
>
> I'm also finding your approach to story structure to be a tremendous help. In short, thank you for your perspective and resources.
>
> ~ Joyce Koch, Winner, Romance Feature Screenplay category – Las Vegas International Film & Screenwriting Festival (2020)

COMPLETE BOOKLIST

Story Stakes

Story Structure for the Win

Story Structure Essentials series

Inciting Incident

Midpoint Magic

Trough of Hell

Story Climax

Iterative Outlining series

Sizzling Story Outlines

Solid Story Compass

Sparkling Story Drafts

Screenwriting Books for Beginners series

How to Write a Screenplay Now

Also Available

Smarter Story Structure (online course)

Christmas Movie Writer Starter Kit (online course)

Printed in Great Britain
by Amazon